From

The Women's Press Ltd
124 Shoreditch High Street, London E1

Barbara Rogers   *Photo by Anita Corbin*

Barbara Rogers has been involved in politics for many years, and
been active in the women's liberation movement. She has written
two books on South Africa, and one on women in the Third World
(*The Domestication of Women: Discrimination in Developing
Societies*).

This is her first opportunity to write the book she has been
planning for a long time: a political view of how women can
organise to get our proper share of decision-making on the issues
that dominate all our lives.

She is an active member of the Labour Party, and a Councillor in
the London Borough of Islington.

BARBARA ROGERS

52%

Getting Women's Power
into Politics

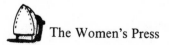 The Women's Press

First published by The Women's Press Limited 1983
A member of the Namara Group
124 Shoreditch High Street, London E1 6JE

British Library Cataloguing in Publication Data

Barbara Rogers
 52%: getting women's power into politics
 1. Women in politics
 I Title
 323.3'4   HQ1236

 ISBN 0-7043-3918-8

Typeset by AKM Associates (UK) Ltd, London
Printed in Great Britain by Nene Litho
and bound by Woolnough Bookbinding,
both of Wellingborough, Northants

Contents

Acknowledgments

I owe a great debt to the Women's Research and Resources Centre and to Sisterwrite bookshop for their wonderful collection of books and articles on just about everything.

Many of the campaigning organisations mentioned in the Resources section of each chapter have provided me with invaluable materials on particular issues, and have given me their time to discuss what they are trying to achieve and how. I am especially grateful for the help provided by the National Council of Women, National Federation of Women's Institutes and the National Union of Townswomen's Guilds.

To all the political organisations and individuals I have worked with and learned from, a big thank you. You may not agree with everything I say, but I hope you will find it a contribution to the political debate.

Thanks finally to the women cartoonists whose work has enlivened the text: Bulbul (p 152 – originally published in *Pulling Our Own Strings*, ed Gloria Kaufman & Mary K Blakely, Indiana University Press); Liz Mackie (pp 22, 73, 99, 137) whose cartoons have appeared in *Sour Cream*, Sheba Feminist Publishers, and in *Spare Rib*); Christine Roche (pp 59 & 112); and Paula Youens (p 13).

Introduction

Women are fed up with politics and politicians. Every appeal is still to 'the man in the street' or 'the average man'. Fifty years of women's right to participate in politics, the subject of bitter struggles by the women's suffrage movement, might as well not have existed for all the relevance to us of today's political 'debate'. We are dismissed as conservative, as stupid, even as following whatever our men tell us, as not knowing our own minds. And at the same time we are the first targets whenever there are public services to be cut, prices to be fixed or taxation to be raised. When there is a need for women in industry, they tell us that is our place; when they do not need us, they decide our place is at home.

It is no surprise that many women have turned their backs on conventional party politics. One-issue campaigns, national and local, have become a focus for our political energies. Yet that very experience has shown the importance of getting involved in the political process itself, covering the whole range of issues. The time has come for many of us when politics has become too important to leave to the men only. The political mess we find ourselves in is threatening our personal lives as well as family and social life as we know it. If we are to get a health service that meets our needs, an education that helps rather than hinders our working life, legislation to outlaw discrimination against us, protection from violence and abuse, reasonable housing, proper care for our small children and elderly relatives, and freedom of movement, speech and expression – then we are going to have to fight for them. The politicians will have to learn how to listen to us for a change. The press and broadcasting media, which play a big role in defining political issues, will have to rethink from our point of view what they really are.

Women complain – constantly – to each other. We are afraid to let the toddler out of the house because of the traffic, angry about our miserable pension or social security rights, about the humiliating experience at the ante-natal clinic or hospital, about men intimidating us in the street, about the school hours and holidays, about the prices we are paying for necessities for our families, about the brush-off we get from the trade unions, about the bomb, about the low pay and insecurity of our jobs. . .

Nobody in a position to do anything about these problems takes much notice. After all, they say, that's only a women's issue.

There have been some significant cases recently where women have mobilised, apparently spontaneously, on issues of concern to us. Enormous pressure has been applied by women all over the country to abolish the tax discrimination against women, sparked off by articles in *Woman's Own* and the *Sunday Times*. That was a challenge to a Labour Government. Later, when the Conservative Government which followed it announced that we would lose our right to live and work in Britain with our families if our husband was born overseas, there was an outburst of anger from women of all kind of political allegiances. In the most significant victory so far, the Corrie Bill against abortion rights was prevented from getting through, despite overwhelming support from the men in Parliament, because of the outburst of fear and anger from women who want the decision to be ours. In each of these cases the men at the top declared themselves amazed by the amount of pressure they were getting, from all over the place. They have not yet understood how deeply we resent their failure to consider our point of view.

In this book I have tried to define women's issues in a new way, as our perspective on *all* issues. Many questions have been raised by the feminist movement – including rape, domestic violence, child-care and abortion – and these are extremely important. However, our perspective has to be wider than this. Problems which have been routinely dismissed as 'purely personal' have to be recognised as political. Politics is not about abstractions, but about the immediate concerns of ordinary voters. As the feminist slogan so aptly expresses it, the personal is political and the political is personal.

There is a great deal that women can do as individuals about some of the problems discussed here, and I have included details of some organisations which provide resources as well as a voice for those wanting to campaign on particular issues. However, many women are moving beyond single-issue campaigns to involvement

2

in political parties where we can be involved in the whole range of the debate. We are trying to bring to this debate a new political awareness among women, and a new understanding among the policy-makers of our perspective on all the issues.

Our support, and our votes, are linked to what *we* want politically – we are tired of supporting a political contest which is all about men. The politicians will be forced to realise, many of them probably for the first time, that we have our own way of looking at the issues and that we can put across our point of view by our political decisions. A woman's vote, when it comes to the count, has exactly the same weight as a man's.

Sisterhood, as we say, is powerful.

1
Money and Jobs

It is taken for granted by politicians that people's votes are determined by the effect of policies on the pockets of the electorate. Governments have poured money into the economy or cut taxes, in election years, in an open attempt to buy public votes. They agonise over levels of inflation, wage settlements, unemployment, public investment, exchange rates, tax, social security and pensions, and the general state of the economy – as the bread and butter of national politics. They are all measured in terms of their effect on 'the average man'.

If the politicians were to stop and think about the women's vote, they would have to see that economic policy geared towards the average man affects women profoundly, and often makes us worse off. The analysis has been ludicrously simplistic so far, with policy-makers apparently unable to go beyond the price of butter as an economic issue that could influence our voting. They do not stop to think, for example, about any possible alternatives to their enormous investment in certain industries which have little impact on women directly – steel, coal-mining, the car industry, and ship and aircraft-building. Were women ever considered in the decision to divert huge sums of public money to developing Concorde? The car industry alone takes millions of pounds out of tax revenue, *our* money, every year, not only in direct subsidies to British Leyland but in the subsidies for company cars which ensure a domestic market for otherwise unsaleable goods. Other vitally important industries which are under pressure, such as the clothing and textile industries which are among the biggest employers in the country, are completely neglected by the economic planners, and promising design and management talent is lost to other countries which see these industries as the big revenue-earners they are.

Another sphere in which women's interests are seen as irrelevant is that of energy policy and particularly the pricing and management of domestic fuel supplies. Staggering amounts of money have been poured into research and development of nuclear power, for example, and a string of uneconomic and probably extremely dangerous nuclear reactors have been constructed around the country. These have greatly benefited the big engineering concerns involved, and created an enormous oversupply of electricity generating capacity, a rapid rise in fuel bills, and a system of draconian powers for the fuel boards to cut off people who cannot pay without any need to go to court or negotiate about the debts. Official interest in domestic insulation and energy conservation, which would be of particular benefit to those women who spend a lot of time at home, is almost non-existent in Britain.

Women are the main victims of an unbalanced energy policy, just as we have to pay for the investment of public funds in sectors which are of no interest or benefit to us.

There is only one aspect of economic policy which is recognised as being of interest to women: prices in general, and food prices in particular. Women very often take responsibility for household budgets for food and other essentials, and are therefore more aware of changes in price and consumer problems in general. It reveals a great deal about the politicians' perception of our judgment that food prices have risen astronomically since the end of the food subsidies and the cheap food policy of the post-war Labour Government. Both the Conservatives and Labour have adopted policies which raised food prices for the benefit of the public exchequer – relieved of food subsidies – and particularly of the farmers. In fact agricultural policy as a whole, which has received so little attention in comparison with industrial policy, is a subject of very direct concern to women. It is generally realised now that the European Economic Community has increased the discrepancy between producers and consumers, responding to the powerful agro-business lobby. However, this is merely a continuation of policies which recent British Governments practised before joining the EEC, in parallel to the Community's Common Agricultural Policy.

Massive subsidies are now going to farm producers to 'mine' the land rather than conserve it for future generations, by draining wetlands, ploughing up grazing, cutting down woods and hedgerows, and replacing rural labour by investment in chemicals and machinery. This has led to the destruction of our countryside and to the erosion of the rural areas' whole economic base. We are all affected by this destructive, macho policy towards the countryside, quite apart from our concern for the price and quality

5

of the foodstuffs produced in this way. The factory farming systems and the cruelty to animals associated with them must also be of concern; the growing movement for animal rights is to a large extent dependent on women who are active on this issue.

Many politicians see women exclusively as 'housewives', but this makes it all the more strange that they have not seen the political issues surrounding our work in the house. National economic statistics and estimates of the active labour force, on which economic planning is based, have systematically failed to account for the value of women's unpaid work. This is work that, if not done at home, would have to be paid for and so is a direct saving of expenditure: child care, social and nursing work for our own relatives, and others helped by us through voluntary organisations; food preparation, clothes-making, the purchase and maintenance of equipment; and other services which would otherwise have to be provided. An estimate of the market value of work done by a woman with children, worked out for insurance companies, is over £200 a week gross. The number of hours spent on housework of all kinds by women is often far in excess of the normal 'working week' of 40 to 45 hours. One survey found that women spent anything between 48 and 105 hours a week on housework, the average time being 78 hours. Despite these very long hours, many of the women were doing paid jobs elsewhere as well, either part-time or full-time. A serious economic crisis is building up for many families, and for individual women, in trying to juggle the number of hours available for work and the income earned, or expenditure saved, as a result of the choices made – both at an individual level and in terms of public policy and planning.

There are many government policies which have a far-reaching influence on the freedom of choice for women about our work, including the availability of child care and respite care for people with disabilities, the opening hours of shops and other facilities, and the tax concessions available for different items of expenditure. For example, falling levels of child benefit may force many women to get a paid job to keep their children, whether they are single mothers, or wives who are not getting a fair share of their husband's pay or social security. The fact that payment for child care in order to get paid work is not counted as a necessary business expense in assessing tax liabilities means that many women are forced to get the cheapest child-minder available or to do all the work themselves, at great cost to their own health and freedom – and perhaps the welfare of the child as well. All these

6

issues have an economic value attached, quite apart from the importance of personal job satisfaction and the self-esteem that depends on doing a job which is acknowledged by other people as valuable. The work that women do, at home and in paid employment, should be a matter of personal choice between a range of alternatives that is not skewed by the irrational economic policies of a government interested only in the pockets of the men. And if the women's areas of housework and voluntary work in the community do become properly valued and supported by government policies wherever possible, then we are likely to find men getting more involved in doing their share of the housework and the voluntary activity. Meanwhile, on the other side of the work coin, policies relating to paid employment have to be seen as crucial economic issues for women, just as much as for men.

Employment policy

Many women have an interest in men's wages, if they are married and have a husband in a good job. But the politicians seem to think that this is our only interest in employment policy, despite the overwhelming majority of women who earn an income in their own right. Policy-makers see the average employee as a married man with a dependent wife, and perhaps children, but less than a quarter (22 percent) of wage-earners come into this category. According to the official statistics at least 41 percent of all wage-earners are women. In fact the proportion is higher since this excludes many part-time and low-paid workers who are women. Many of us have dependants of our own, and increasing numbers of women are responsible for families where there is no father to act as 'breadwinner'. Even in two-parent families, the mother's wages are often essential. The Department of Health and Social Security (DHSS) has estimated that the number of families living in poverty would treble if the women in them did not have a paid job, bringing another $2\frac{1}{2}$ million families into the poverty levels where they require Family Income Supplement. Even though 40 percent of the women included in official labour statistics are working only part-time it is estimated that a third of the married women are making a major contribution to the family income: between a third and a half. Our contribution to all household budgets is rising considerably, as the proportion of women in the work force rises towards the number of men. Marriage is no longer, by itself, a bar to seeking paid work, since the same proportion of married and e women are now in the paid labour force.

Statistics can show the importance of women's wages, but the employment issue goes far beyond mere numbers. There are very few women of working age in this country who are not either in a paid job, looking for one, or prevented from doing so by a full-time unpaid job such as looking after small children or people with disabilities. Job prospects, pay and conditions are of crucial importance to us not just in managing on a day-to-day basis, but as the basis for planning our whole working life.

Women seek jobs for the same reason that men do – for the money. At the same time, since money determines our own personal standing in the community, having a job can be vital to our self-esteem. Being unemployed, for whatever reason, can be devastating to our health and general well-being. It has been found that men who are made redundant suffer from the same symptoms of depression, anxiety and feelings of worthlessness that afflict so many 'housewives' without jobs. Recent research has shown that women are most likely to be happy if they have a good job, 'the single factor that correlates most closely with a woman's sense of self-esteem', as the jargon has it. This factor is much more important to women's well-being than being married or having children, despite the romantic myths about the fulfilled wife and mother. For mental health and social involvement, we need to have useful work and to have that work recognised as important in the common currency of our whole society – money. It is well known that women who could afford to stay out of work are often anxious to get jobs, as a way of saving their sanity as much as for the money. Women who do not have paid jobs, but usually work very hard for nothing, also need to have their value properly recognised, financially as well as socially, and this is something that we will consider separately.

Since paid employment is so vitally important to us, it shows almost unbelievable insensitivity when politicians advocate forcing us out of our jobs. This is a favourite theme of Conservative Party men in particular. Keith Joseph, for example, on becoming Secretary of State for Education, announced that we should all quit our jobs, 'I'm not in the least shy about being old fashioned'. Patrick Jenkin suggested, 'If the good Lord had intended us to have equal rights to go out to work, he wouldn't have created men and women'.

A Conservative peer, Lord Spens, explained that we were not going to be let off work, but we should no longer be paid for it: 'I am not saying they should not be occupied – just that they should not compete in the market for paid jobs'. Margaret Thatcher, who has rejected this stern advice for herself, then complains that women fail because 'they are not naturally ambitious enough'.

Conservative Party policy has in fact been built on its neanderthal attitudes towards women's jobs. The whole 'family policy' has been largely directed at undermining our bargaining power in the work-place: cutting nursery and child-care provision, sending old and disabled people back home and reducing the value of child benefit.

The 1980 Employment Act, which was advertised mainly as a union-bashing exercise, was actually far more effective in its removal of women's rights at work. It abolished important rights to maternity leave and maternity pay, to much needed kinds of protection for the position of part-time workers, and to claims for unfair dismissal. It also abolished Schedule 11 of the 1975 Employment Protection Act, which was designed to improve the wages of low-paid workers. Throughout the life of the first Thatcher Government, vast numbers of jobs were eliminated in the public sector where women predominate, especially in the social services, health services, education, the lower ranks of the civil service and work for local authorities. Although there has been virtually no publicity for their plight, school catering workers have suffered more redundancies than the heavily publicised steel-workers.

Redundancies among women have become an even more serious problem than for men. Between 1975 and 1980 official unemployment among women more than trebled, as compared to a rise of 50 percent among men – although the two are not directly comparable because the women's figures are officially recorded at a much lower level than the men's. Millions of women without jobs are not being registered as unemployed where they do not qualify for unemployment benefit, and the definitions are very blurred as a result. It seems that women's official unemployment rates are only half the actual numbers of redundancies among women: it takes the loss of two women's jobs for the figures to record the loss of one. In addition to this are the millions of women who would like to have a job, but give up looking because they have so little hope of finding anything appropriate to their skills because of the jobs shortage. If all such women were recognised officially as unemployed, the true extent of women's unemployment would become apparent: it is about the same number of women as men.

9

This *excludes* the millions more women who would like to get a job but are prevented by the lack of government support for their family and community work.

Unemployment is a women's issue just as much as a men's one, if not more so. Yet, as we have seen, the Conservative Government has actually 'cooked' the figures to disguise the numbers of jobless women officially recognised. And the Labour Party, although it upholds a 'woman's right to work' (perhaps we would prefer the right to *paid* work) still attacks this issue almost exclusively in terms of men's unemployment.

Women need to become far more aware of unemployment as an issue for us, and also much more assertive in putting forward our own point of view. Far too many men in powerful positions, from trade union officials and employers to the politicians at every level, believe that they can solve men's unemployment by driving women out of our jobs. A sample survey of opinion done in 1980 by Market and Opinion Research International (MORI) for the *New Statesman* showed that in fact a clear majority of men (46 percent to 38 percent) rejected the idea that 'where jobs are scarce, married women should be discouraged from working'. This probably reflects the importance of women's wages to so many of the families these men belong to, as well as a basic sense of justice that does them credit. Among women surveyed, twice as many rejected this idea as agreed with it (50 percent to 28 percent). Whilst it was the male white-collar workers who were most supportive of women having the same right to a job, manual workers were evenly divided; and among the women questioned, social class made no difference at all to their feelings on this issue.

Pay and conditions at work

Legislation and regulations about employment are extremely complicated, and the whole policy needs to be thoroughly overhauled both in detail and in principle to reflect women's interests and give us a fair deal at work. There is, however, one issue which has had very little discussion as a women's issue, but should be one of the most important for us: the protection of workers in low-wage sectors and industries by the introduction of a national minimum wage. Since the great majority of employees working for the lowest wages are women, including part-time workers and homeworkers, the introduction of a statutory minimum wage would be of immediate benefit to us. This applies not only to those at the very bottom, but also those stuck in all the low-paid jobs. The minimum wage would act as a floor level, from which we can then negotiate with whatever organisational force we can get for improvements. The absence of any minimum means that low-paid workers are constantly in danger of being undercut by those working for even less.

Politically, the idea of a statutory minimum wage is extremely contentious. The trade unions are split on the issue, with unions like the National Union of Public Employees (NUPE) representing low-paid workers, fighting hard for a minimum wage against the entrenched power of the exclusive craft unions which are mainly interested in using their muscle against employers without interference from the State, and insisting on 'differentials' which keep the gap between their wages and the lower-paid as wide as possible. If the argument for greater equality and for priority to go to the worst-off is to win through in the trade unions, it is going to have to be through women making this one of our main demands, both at the work place and in the whole political process.

The present system for fixing minimum wages in different industries is through the Wages Councils, a very complex system set up in the 1920s to protect workers not covered by collective bargaining. It is not working well because of the failure of the Government to enforce Wages Council rulings. The Low Pay Unit and others have estimated that two million women are being paid less than the legal minimum for their industry, with nearly 11,000 employers cheating us out of £28 million a year. The number of inspectors has never been adequate, and under the Conservatives it has been cut to the bone: each inspector is now supposed to deal with 3,000 firms at a time. Only nine prosecutions were undertaken in 1981, and the small fines that resulted were negligible in comparison with the money saved by paying less than the legal minimum. Many of the women surveyed by the Low Pay Unit were being paid much less than the level of supplementary benefit – supposedly the minimum required to buy the necessities of life. Some women surveyed in Leicester were found to be doing 'outwork' as sub-contractors to the companies at the rate of 10p an hour in 1981. It appears that far from trying to protect women from exploitation at work, the Conservative Government has been planning to abolish the Wages Councils altogether; they are kept nominally in operation because of Britain's commitment to a Convention of the International Labour Organisation, expiring in 1985, which calls for the protection of low-paid workers.

It is indeed a ludicrous situation, and one which the Conservatives are pledged to eliminate, that people can earn less by taking paid work than the minimum to which they are entitled as supplementary benefit when they are unemployed. The women receiving a wage less than the SB level actually include a number working directly for the Government's own Civil Service, mainly as cleaners. With a serious economic recession and massive redundancies and cost-cutting by the employers, women are far too easy to use as cheap labour, and it is in the interests of all workers – men as well as women – to look at the problems of undercutting by women and, in some industries, by children. The parallels with Victorian times are all too painfully obvious. Setting a national minimum wage, at substantially above supplementary benefit levels, is becoming an essential safeguard for the benefit of all wage-earners. Women, who are concentrated in sectors such as textiles, retailing, clerical work, the health service, catering and cleaning, as well as the bottom end of many other economic sectors, will have to lead the fight for a minimum living wage.

There is, at the same time, the even more basic question of why and how women are being confined to the lowest-paid jobs with the least security and promotion prospects. The whole question of discrimination in the employment field is very much a women's issue, and one that has attracted a great deal of attention from the Equal Opportunities Commission (EOC) and campaigning organisations. The two pioneering pieces of legislation in this area are the Equal Pay Act and the Sex Discrimination Act, both of which came into effect in 1975, introduced by the Labour Government to mark International Women's Year. They have now been tested and evaluated, and substantial changes are necessary to make the law fully effective in combating discrimination at work.

The effect of the two Acts on women's employment prospects has in fact been disappointing. The overwhelming majority of us are trapped in mainly female jobs at low rates: employers have made sure that we have no man in the same grade, or doing the same work, with whom we can claim equal pay. The *Sunday Times* discovered in 1973 that the Employers' Federations were advising their members that where 'conflict' might arise, that is, women demanding their new legal rights to equal pay for the same or similar work, the women involved should be sacked and replaced either by men or by machines. Justification could be found by making a big issue out of any lateness or absences from work. They urged separate job structures for women and men, to avoid claims

IF I'M YOUR
BETTER HALF
WHY'S MY PAY
A QUARTER THE
SIZE OF YOURS?..

Youens

of equal work. One memorandum leaked to the paper showed that evasion of the Equal Pay Act was a deliberate strategy on the part of the employers' organisations:

> Where job evaluation is used it may be possible to minimise the impact of equal pay by changing the work content of women's jobs significantly so that re-evaluation is justified. Alternatively the withdrawal of men or women from certain jobs in the existing job structure may limit the scope for parity claims.

The result was usually to 'freeze' women even more than before in grades which are for women only, with no promotion avenues to better and easier jobs held by the men. A study by the Department of Employment published in December 1981 showed that after initial gains in de-segregating jobs and narrowing the pay difference between women and men in the mid-1970s, the situation has become rapidly worse and in many ways even more unequal than before the two main Acts were passed to try and achieve equality. In 1966, just over half (52 percent) of all women's jobs were in only three service industries. By 1978, according to Labour Research, this figure had risen to 58 percent. The largest sector, with over a quarter of all the women (27 percent), was professional and scientific services, which include typists, secretaries, technicians, teachers and nurses. Next were the distributive trades, with jobs in shops, mail order and warehouses, with 16 percent of all women employed, followed closely by 'miscellaneous services', including laundries, catering, dry cleaning and hairdressing, with 15 percent.

This pattern of restricted choice is in stark contrast to the enormously varied fields open to men, with no industry accounting for even as much as 10 percent of all male workers.

At middle and senior levels we are not only failing to make significant advances in many sectors – including teaching, the civil service and local government – but the proportion of women in higher positions is falling as those who retire are not being replaced by younger women coming up through the ranks. This is very much a political issue, since senior jobs are also those with decision-making powers. The tiny numbers of women in Parliament and in local Councils are fully in line with this negative trend for women's participation in all policy-making positions. There are of course a few well-publicised exceptions to the rule, but the advancement of a Margaret Thatcher or an Anna Ford should not blind us to the fact of their increasing isolation in a growing army of men. The 'first woman train driver' or 'first woman carpenter', while welcome news, should not distract our attention from the continuing concentration of most women into the same old jobs.

To a large extent it is workers themselves who have to organise for their rights: that is the way it always has been, and will continue to be despite repeated attempts to control the labour market through legislation. The trade unions are absolutely crucial institutions for women who want to work for a fair deal from employers, including the elimination of discrimination, and this is the subject of the next chapter. The most that political action can do is to reinforce the basic principles of equal treatment. The National Council for Civil Liberties (NCCL) has set out a number of legal reforms which could be of help to women organising for better jobs.

Perhaps the most important change being suggested by the NCCL is to combine the legislation on sex discrimination and equal pay into one law, in order to allow a woman to claim equal pay with a man if he were to do the same job. She could compare herself with a 'hypothetical man' in her position for claiming equal pay, just as she can now in cases under the Sex Discrimination Act. Combining the two laws would be of special benefit to women in part-time work, who have no full-time male workers doing the same or similar job with whom they can compare their hourly rates. At present, part-time workers on low hourly rates are also unable to make a claim under the Sex Discrimination Act because it does not cover pay.

The second proposal is to amend the Equal Pay Act to provide equal pay for work of equal value - a matter of elementary justice which is not provided for under the present law. The Government has been forced now to concede this principle by a ruling of the EEC Court in 1982. A panel of experts is being established for this purpose by the advisory service ACAS.

These proposals for improving the pay and conditions of women in our existing jobs are vitally important as the only way to bring real employment benefits to large numbers of women, with priority to those in the worst situations. Supplementing these measures should be stronger action to allow women access to the whole range of jobs from which we are excluded at present, through a strengthening of the positive action procedures introduced in the Sex Discrimination Act.

The idea of positive action – or affirmative action as it is called in the United States – is to compensate for present and past discrimination by providing guaranteed access for women into training and job opportunities, if necessary by special programmes for women only. Similar opportunities are being demanded by men in training and employment from which they have been barred: midwifery and secretarial work, for instance. But since men, as we have seen, have a much better range of job options than women, any positive action programme to eliminate discrimination will have to be geared far more to helping women than men. Politically this is a very sensitive issue, and one that women will have to fight for in the face of accusations that we are asking for 'reverse discrimination'. I would suggest that as a matter of tactics we should not be deflected from the aim of real equality of opportunity by accepting token privileges for a few women that can then be used to justify the men's advantages in more important areas. There are in any case great dangers for us in any apparent 'favouritism' of a woman who is not qualified for a job: if she has problems they can be used as an argument that discrimination against women is justified.

The term 'positive discrimination' is quite widely used, often to mean positive action, but it is a misleading term. Discrimination is bad: positive discrimination is a contradiction in terms. The action needed is to redress all past and present discrimination in order to provide equal opportunities to everybody to fulfil their personal potential. (Exactly the same principle applies to providing new opportunities to members of ethnic minorities who have poor job prospects now because of discrimination in the past.) Special encouragement, training, recruitment and promotion for women have the sole function of providing a way in to fields and skills which are now monopolised by those who have already received those kinds of facilities. A great deal of ground has to be made up to get women on to the promotion ladder in all fields, public and private, that will eventually mean our fair share of decision-making, and guarantee that our interests are taken care of as a matter of course and not require yet another campaign to get access to men's opportunities.

There is one particular area that will need to be tackled if we are to make progress in this way, and that is the relationship between women and men at work. There has been surprisingly little attention paid to the personal difficulties faced by many women who are trying to do their job in a co-operative way with men. Harassment is a common occurence. But at last sexual harassment in the work place is being talked about, and women are expressing their anger and distress regarding unwanted touching and propositioning at work. A few trade unions, notably the National Association of Local Government Officers (NALGO), have a policy of confronting sexual harassment and are starting to work out procedures for dealing with it. We should now put this issue into the context of the whole range of strategies sometimes used by men who feel threatened by the equality of women, or by white people who pick on their black colleagues, which is far too often dismissed as 'normal office bullying' or a figment of the victim's imagination. The person involved can be isolated, constantly criticised and undermined, or even threatened with physical violence. It is up to women to support each other when one becomes the target of such a campaign at work, but in many cases there also needs to be recourse to a tribunal or court of law. Careful study is needed of the ways in which complaints of harassment can be effectively, speedily and seriously dealt with by the trade unions, employers and where necessary the courts. Far too often the 'solution' to a problem of this kind is to fire the victim, as allegedly the cause of the trouble, or to force her to leave. This is often the culmination of a long period of acute distress. This kind of thing is a much more powerful way than we have so far recognised of keeping women in the safe 'female ghetto' of the low-paid sectors and the lower ranks of all sectors.

The range of employment issues which are of special interest to women is very wide, and much more attention needs to be paid to all of them by women and by the organised labour movement, the trade unions, which are powerful political bodies in their own right in direct dealings with the Government as well as with individual employers. Many of women's interests at work can best be dealt with in the framework of collective bargaining with employers through trade unions. Changes in employment law, regardless of which party is in power, depend largely on the positions taken by the trade union movement. For real progress towards a fair deal at work, then, women in the trade union movement are calling on us to fight for much more influence within our unions. The trade unions too can retain their influence only if they adapt to the needs of the increasing proportion of their members who are women, and who at the moment are not being properly represented.

Resources

Job discrimination and low pay cases are the responsibility of the Equal Opportunities Commission, Overseas House, Quay Street, Manchester M3 3HN (tel: 061-833 9244). The EOC also has a number of publications on the issues involved.

The best research on low pay in various sectors is available from the Low Pay Unit, 9 Poland Street, London W1. Among its pamphlets are *Women: Work and Wages*, available at £1.20.

As on many issues, the National Council for Civil Liberties is an excellent campaigning organisation, working through its Rights for Women Unit. A key contribution to the debate on job discrimination is *Positive Action for Women: the next step in education, training and employment* by Sadie Robarts with Anna Coote and Elizabeth Ball, 1981, at £2. The NCCL also has pamphlets on maternity rights, shift work and other issues relating to women's employment, including *Amending the Equality Laws*, 1983, price 95p. The address is 21 Tabard Street, London SE1.

For an insight into harassment of women at work see Michael Korda's *Male Chauvinism! How it works – the truth at last*, published in paperback by Ballantine Books, New York, 1973.

2
Are the Trade Unions Our Unions?

The excuses commonly heard from trade union activists and officials about their weakness in organising and representing working women sound like a litany of men's insults to women. We are 'difficult' to organise. Our wages are not important, they are 'pin money'. Our responsibility for dependants – children, husbands, parents and others – far from being the basis for protecting our earnings, is the excuse for agreements with management to get rid of us. In our desperate search for a job that will be compatible with the demands of these dependants on our time and energies, we form a large part-time and homeworking sector which they see as a 'threat' to the men. According to them we are physically and mentally weak. We undermine 'the lads on the shop floor'. We make unreasonable demands. Our 'place' is at the kitchen sink. By seeking paid work we threaten the claim for a 'family wage' to be paid to men only.

One trade union official tells me he cringes whenever one of his male colleagues starts asking what the union can do to recruit more women, and organise us effectively. This is usually a cue for the repetition of prejudices about women at work, an exercise in 'blame the victim' which then suggests that it is quite impossible to involve women in the trade unions, despite all the evidence to the contrary.

The history of the trade union movement is complex, based partly on the fight for privilege and partly on the fight against privilege. The craft unions, successors to the Guild system of journeymen and masters, led the way in the early years of the industrial revolution and still tend to dominate much trade union activity. For them, it was a matter of getting rid of workers who threatened their own skilled members, the unskilled or unqualified, women, and part-timers. A 'skilled man' was, by definition, a full-time worker with many years of continuous employment as well as membership of the union. And over the years the criteria to keep him efficient as a 'skilled man' have not changed that much. His position needs constant reinforcement, at work and in regard to his family, since he cannot break his work record by taking the time to care for children or other dependants: almost his only contribution to the family is in the form of cash. In return for whatever part of his wage-packet he chooses to hand over, he expects a level of personal service, especially from his wife, that no normal wage would buy. There is no limit to her hours of work, no holiday, and no retirement. She takes total responsibility for all family and household problems and crises. It is only the services of a wife, or another woman performing the same service, that makes possible the working and social life of a 'skilled man'. Anyone who takes even partial responsibility for others is almost automatically excluded from that life.

Since they organised, working men have had two areas of privilege to protect. The first is their position at work, where they are demanding better jobs, higher wages, and all obtainable fringe benefits, at the expense of those who threaten 'dilution' of those privileges. The second is within their own families, where they want 'freedom' from any obligations even to be at home if they do not want to be, let alone to do any of the work. In both cases, they are effectively organising for restrictions on women's freedom, our relegation to the lowest-paid and worst work – or none at all – and our obligation to provide domestic service.

The story of trade union struggles contains within it a history of working men organising against working women, demanding our expulsion from whole areas of employment which in fact has meant confining us to female 'ghettoes' such as domestic work, the health service, light engineering, parts of the textile industry, and clerical work. During the two World Wars, women were drawn into munitions and heavy engineering work in huge numbers, and without women the country could not have sustained the war effort. Immediately afterwards, however, the men organised systematically to evict the women from most of those jobs, especially the skilled ones; they closed down the multitude of work place nurseries set up during the Second World War, and forced women into the low-pay ghettoes, part-time work, homeworking and outright unemployment. The effects of these efforts are visible almost everywhere: the Union of Communications Workers (UCW), for example, has made sure that women do not deliver the mail, and the Transport and General Workers (TGWU) has effectively excluded women from driving buses – with a very few recent exceptions. The all important apprenticeships, controlled by the craft unions, are almost entirely closed to women. Men in the trade unions actively conspired with the men in management to frustrate the Equal Pay Act, first by agreeing to 'phase in' equal pay with long delays but even more importantly by tying it to various forms of regrading exercises, where all the women in many work places would be confined to one or perhaps two all-women grades.

At times of recession, like the present, women's jobs are not only restricted, they are also very vulnerable. Research carried out in West Germany as well as Britain by Friedrich Weltz shows a strong tendency for trade unions to concentrate power in the hands of a core of full-time men with long service, while 'marginal' workers are forced out during any period of recession and forced redundancies. Management is happy to collude in this, since the 'marginal' workers have little chance of organising effectively against it, and in any event they are easily replaced when business picks up again. They are mainly women – especially the part-timers – but other groups badly affected are disabled people, members of ethnic or religious minorities who face discrimination and may have broken through into employment only recently, and also the older workers over 45 who have no protection from discrimination on grounds of age. Generally speaking, on the principle of 'last in, first out' it is those people who have faced discrimination in getting work in the first place, or whose choice of work has been restricted by dependent relatives and children, who are the first to be fired. Again, we see the pattern of privilege being established, at the expense of the most desperate members of the labour force – and trade unions as the organisational framework for this.

Women fight back

While it is important to recognise trade unions as instruments of discrimination against women, history also shows us that women can, and do, use trade union organisation to make our demands effective. In order to do this, however, we have to be very clear about the kinds of obstacles that we face. The unions, in turn, have to realise that they need women as full participants in order to grow in the face of economic disaster and political attack.

In the last few years, unemployment has been rising alarmingly. Many trade union members have been made redundant, and almost all of these then leave the union, despite some efforts to provide services to unemployed members. Trade union numbers would have fallen substantially as a result, if it had not been for the major expansion in union activity among white-collar workers, and in the service industries generally. Overwhelmingly, the workers involved are women. Since 1961 total union membership has doubled, to a total of around 13.5 million people, although this is now a relatively static figure. From being only a fifth of the membership of TUC-affiliated unions in 1961, twenty years later women formed almost a third – a massive increase not only in the proportion of trade union membership, but even more dramatically in the *numbers* of women involved. In 1980 the total number of women in the unions was over 4 million, three times the number in 1961.

A crucial element in this relationship is the considerable scope which still exists for extending trade union membership and organisation among women workers, and especially the 3 million part-timers and the perhaps half a million home-workers. Research consistently shows that many women in both categories would like to join a trade union to protect their interests in bargaining with employers, but are prevented by the total absence of any contact with union representatives. Union membership among all women is still much lower than among men, as is shown by the fact that the number of women in paid jobs outside our homes is approaching the number of men, while our union membership is less than half that of men. In a 1980 MORI poll, only 28 percent of the employed women interviewed said they belonged to a union, compared with 53 percent of the men. The lowest figures of all were among the part-timers, almost all of them women, of whom only 19 percent belonged to a union. Other categories of workers where women had low participation rates were those over 45, manual workers (there was relatively little difference between women and men among white-collar workers) and those between the ages of 25 and 34, when there are likely to be small children involved.

This is the crucial age for women as far as our working lives are concerned. Men are obviously becoming fathers in this age group in about the same numbers, yet their parental responsibilities are very much secondary to the demands of their employment. Women, both those with husbands or live-in partners and those who form one-parent families, are left holding the baby and are at enormous disadvantage at work as a result. It is in this age-group that women form the smallest proportion of the total work force, despite the fact that this should be the most formative period of a

21

working life, and women in this young age-group are forced into the part-time sector, with all its disadvantages and insecurity. Even those who have a full-time job are less likely to belong to a trade union than women of any other age-group. The effect of all these barriers, at this crucial early stage of women's working life, is that only one-twentieth of those involved have a full-time job and belong to a trade union, compared with half the men in the same age group.

Men's participation in unions as fully-fledged full-timers, at a stage when experience is being gained and influence developed, is *ten times* that of women. The result is seen for the rest of a worker's life: a typical male trade unionist in his late thirties or forties, the age when real power is being acquired in union affairs, will have 'served his time' with 20 years of steady work and union activity. A typical woman might be just getting started, after interruptions, changes of job and perhaps part-time work or unemployment, leaving little or no time for union affairs.

The failure to recruit so many employed women is clearly a problem for the trade unions: they are losing out on total numbers, and therefore on organisational and financial strength in relation both to employers and to the Government, which is the focus of much union activity at the national level. The rigid pattern of recruitment and advancement within the union structure, geared to the work patterns of men, serves as a barrier to the unions in general in organising many sectors of the economy which are using part-time, temporary or home-workers. In allowing whole sectors to remain unorganised and extremely low-paid, the unions are helping to undermine the bargaining position of all workers. Strictly in trade union terms, then, there is an obvious need to recruit women and involve them fully in organisation at the work

"CALL A MEETING ON WOMEN AFTER WORK & WHAT HAPPENS? ONLY TWO TURN UP. WHERE WERE THEY ALL, I'D LIKE TO KNOW"

place. But what about women? Do we really need trade unions as much as they need us?

Many women would respond negatively to this question, based on their experience of unions being men's clubs which not only organise against women's interests at work, but show no scruples about using forms of industrial action which, although aimed at the employer, have a very serious impact on women. Public services such as transport, gas and electricity, the schools and health services are essential for women's major, unpaid work: housework and the care of dependants. Women do in fact tend to be more hostile to trade unions than men, and this became a factor in the 1978 'Winter of Discontent' that so damaged the Labour Government. Women picketed male pickets outside schools, demonstrated against strikers, and at one factory female employees attacked male lorry-drivers who were picketing. The popular press certainly manipulated the women's actions to attack the Labour Government and all trade unions indiscriminately, and one cannot condone this. However, the fact that the women's attacks on union activities took place at all, spontaneous as they were, should be cause for great concern in the trade unions about their anti-women image, at a time when they are still under serious political attack from other quarters.

In the MORI poll already mentioned, women were more critical than men of the role and powers of trade unions in general. Interestingly enough, actual membership of a union had more impact on women's attitudes than on men's – if they were members they were more likely than other women to identify with the need for strong union organisation, whereas the difference between union and non-union men was less marked.

Large-scale recruitment of women into trade unions, and an increased concern for our needs as unpaid as well as paid workers, can have a radicalising effect in political terms which will only strengthen the trade union movement and the Labour Party. In the MORI poll a clear connection between anti-union and anti-Labour attitudes was suggested, with two-thirds of the women in the sample agreeing that the Labour Party should not be so closely linked to the unions, as opposed to just over half of the men. The Conservative Party's campaign for the 1979 General Election exploited this connection brilliantly, with attacks on the trade union men combined with pictures of Mrs Thatcher washing up, doing the shopping and looking after children. The fact that she actually does little or no real housework, and has no concern for working women – paid or unpaid – did not detract from the carefully manipulated television image. That lesson was learned only *after* thousands of women had switched their votes to someone they thought would, at last, understand their problems.

Women do need trade unions, unions which will adequately represent our interests, and utilise our own knowledge and experience about problems at the work place and the closely related problems inside our homes and in society generally. The extreme segregation of women into certain sectors and certain grades means that we are an obvious target for redundancies where these are being negotiated by men for men.

Many areas of women's employment are being threatened by new technologies such as the use of micro-computers. Clerical and office work could be completely reorganised and de-skilled by employers, eliminating or effectively demoting the many thousands of women involved. One study in West Germany, which suggests that over 40 percent of existing office work could be done by machines, would indicate the strong possibility of 2 million unemployed clerks and typists in Britain. Negotiating the way in which the new technology is to be introduced, and protecting the position of workers faced with personal disaster arising from redundancy, is a crucial function of the trade unions which is particularly important to women trapped in a sector threatened in this way, with no plans being made for their retraining or redeployment. A related problem (on which APEX, the clerical union, has done some work) is the health hazard caused by some of the new machinery, including eye damage from Visual Display Units, stress from too rapid work and cancer from new chemicals, all of these in addition to the many health hazards found in offices, as in other areas where women are concentrated, which the trade unions have failed to tackle as vigorously as the health and safety problems in industry which mainly affect men.

There are many areas where women need trade union representation, covering the whole field of conventional work on wages and fringe benefits, plus the special needs of women as particularly desperate job-seekers, as having sole responsibility for children, and as disadvantaged workers who have a history of discrimination reaching back to our school-days. We need child-care facilities, for example, parental leave, protection from sexual harassment, and full access to training at all levels with time off as necessary, on equal terms with men. Ideally, there would be special training courses for women to make up for those we have missed through past discrimination.

Discrimination itself can most effectively be tackled by collective bargaining with an employer rather than by individual legal action. Trade unions can refer equal pay issues to the CAC which is well placed to carry out an evaluation of women's jobs in the context of the overall pay structure. Despite some limitation on the CACs by the High Court ruling of 1979, there is still scope for useful work. However, legal action is no substitute for direct negotiation between trade unions and management in establishing reasonable working conditions in a particular company or industry. The most spectacular successes for women in the struggle for equal pay have resulted from strikes, for example, at the Trico factory in West London, at the Nettle engineering factory in Stockport, and at the neighbouring Bowbros Ltd. All received backing from the union involved as well as the wider trade union and women's movements. The Equal Pay Act itself, the objective of a long campaign, was given a major boost by an unofficial women's strike at Ford's Dagenham plant, directed as much against the TWGU as against the management. Substantial advances have been made for women in the public sector as a result of good union organisation, with the result that our wages in manual occupations outside the male preserve of the manufacturing industry have improved, against the overall trend of renewed decline in women's earnings compared with men's generally.

Trade unions can tackle the problems of women at many different levels, and not merely in the work place. Many of them are affiliated to the Labour Party, and effectively control its policy through their votes at conference. They sponsor Labour candidates, who are expected to press for the interests of their members and for union policies in Parliament. Trade union representatives participate in many influential public bodies on a local and national level, including the boards of nationalised industries, and unions are constantly lobbying government departments over employment related issues, major and minor, on behalf of their membership. There is a strong case for increasing the scope of trade union policy involvement so that it is not confined to the problems of people only in relation to their employers, but looks also at the closely related policy issues of child care and the whole 'social wage' – social security, the health service and public services in general – which is of such immense importance to all women. It was not long ago that the trade unions were instrumental in wrecking a Labour Government's proposal to increase the rate of child benefit to be paid to women. With that kind of history, some kind of revolution may be needed in the trade union hierarchies in order for them to be able to represent women adequately. As the Women's TUC reported for the year 1978/79:

> Some trade unions have not yet appreciated that . . . the remarkable and rapid increase in women's membership of unions is more revolutionary than evolutionary, and that as such it requires a new approach.

Positive action in the trade unions

There is no shortage of suggestions for ways of recruiting and involving women in trade unions, as part of a positive action programme to correct the cumulative effects of discrimination over the course of recent industrial history. They include special training courses for women, our appointment as shop stewards especially where groups of women workers are concerned, and our participation as union organisers and officials, as well as representing the union on delegations to major meetings of all kinds. The emphasis on 'serving your time', which only male trade unionists can do, would have to be scrapped in favour of a focus on direct representation of all elements of the work force, including younger workers, older ones who may have had many years spent elsewhere, newly unionised workers, and of course the part-timers and home-workers. If this were the pattern of representation, it would open up new avenues to long deprived groups of workers including women, all black people, the disabled, younger workers – and even perhaps the unemployed.

A recent case involving part-timers indicates that there is already strong pressure on the trade unions to abandon their entrenched bias towards the able-bodied white men who work full-time, often with compulsory overtime, for many years without a break – a soul-destroying pattern of working life that many of the men would like to escape if they could. A 24-year-old woman, Sandra Powell, won an important discrimination case in December 1981 with the claim that the agreement between the trade union and the management of her company to fire part-time workers first during lay-offs had discriminated against her and her family, for which she was an essential breadwinner. The tribunal ruled that the agreement imposed a condition, that they should be full-time workers, which the majority of working women would be unable to fulfil because of their responsibilities for small children. The NCCL pointed out immediately afterwards that this ruling made all union and management agreements penalising part-time workers illegal.

Generally speaking, the NCCL's research shows that part-timers generally, estimated to constitute 40 percent of all female workers, are becoming much more outspoken in defence of their threatened position in the work force. The Low Pay Unit too has observed that once effectively organised, part-time workers are likely to become extremely militant as the struggle of various groups of cleaners has shown in recent years. NUPE has achieved this by making a particular effort to recruit and organise part-timers. Their membership increased by 241 percent between 1966 and 1977. Lesser gains have also been made by two other unions in the public sector, NALGO and the Confederation of Health Service Employees (COHSE). As already noted, the combined effort of these three unions has resulted in a substantial improvement in pay and conditions for women in manual work in the public sector. By contrast, the Low Pay Unit found that part-timers in other sectors saw their relevant unions as being hostile to them, an accurate perception, since many unions, or their individual organisers, will not accept part-time workers as members. Several of the old craft unions are actively opposed to the employment of part-timers, seeing them as 'diluting' the jobs of the men. As a result of this attitude, many companies which use mainly part-time workers remain completely unorganised, and the workers there are under the almost total control of management with very poor wages and conditions.

The TUC, in its statement 'Aims for Women at Work' included in its 1977 Charter, has agreed that 'part-time workers should receive pay and conditions at least pro rata to the full-time workers with whom they work'. Here is in fact the basis for a resolution to the trade unions' hostility to part-timers, which has been linked to their dislike of employers being able to take on cheap labour. During the 1970s, with the number of full-time jobs dwindling, the part-time labour force increased substantially, largely because employers could save money this way. Trade unions, instead of practising a rather futile discrimination against part-timers that merely serves to concentrate them in part-time ghettoes, should be giving a high priority to organising them on the basis of fighting for equal pay and fringe benefits with full-timers in proportion to the number of hours worked. Industries which undercut the labour market by employing part-timers at cut rates, such as hotel chains and breweries, should be the target of special recruitment drives by the relevant unions.

Part-time work has many advantages to both employers and employees, with many workers available only on this basis as long as men's full-time commitments and lack of adequate child-care facilities keep women tied to the home in order to look after the children. Part-time work would not disappear from the scene if it were paid fairly, but it would no longer threaten to undercut unionised workers. In time, part-time work on an equal basis with full-time work could become sufficiently attractive to men – especially the fathers of young children – so that some would start to opt for this, at least for short periods. The benefit to children who gain a real father, and of course to their mothers, would be enormous and could begin the long process of freeing younger women for a real choice of employment. Already there is strong pressure inside the trade union movement for the conversion of overtime into new jobs, and for an overall reduction in working hours, both of which would contribute to the process of liberating men as well as women, and increasing the total number of jobs available.

Most of the top trade union leaders, having 'served their time' more than most, have rigidly entrenched views about child-care and home responsibilities being 'women's work'. Their full-time regional organisers do such excessively long hours of work that they often find themselves in great conflict with their wives over child-care and other work around the house, so are unlikely to be sympathetic to the need for more balance: indeed, many of them are separated or divorced from their wives and notably hostile to women in general, as a result. There has been vicious name-calling and jeering from the men at many trade union conferences where women's issues have been raised. It is still being claimed in trade union debates that women's wages are 'pin money' – a gross insult to all their women members. We still have a long way to go, brother.

Some hard bargaining will be necessary in order to get trade unions to represent our needs properly. The notorious case of the Bolton onion-peelers illustrates the problem. The women concerned in a particular company organised themselves very effectively, and started forcing the management to accept a variety of

demands which included such unconventional proposals as flexible hours and split part-time shifts so that the work could be conveniently matched to the school-day of their children. Unable to handle these demands, which were backed by the full work force, the management in desperation called in the union. The union solved the problem for them by recruiting the women. They imposed on the women a routine of inconvenient meetings and heavy union procedures; and formulated the problem in conventional union terms, such as job gradings, which did not relate to the women's greatest needs. This dissipated the force for real change, and the management had no more trouble.

Trade unions are in fact very conservative institutions, and their procedures need challenging. One particularly strong tradition in many of them is that branch meetings usually take place in the evenings, often in pubs or other surroundings which can be alien to women, and well away from the work place. This is based on the unions' strong resistance to allowing management any control over their meetings, for example over the length of time involved. The pattern makes participation almost impossible for most women, however, both in terms of their time spent out of the house when the children are there and with the added problems of transport late at night, unfamiliarity with the union procedures, and the remaining taboo in some areas on women going into pubs on their own. There is nothing to stop workers negotiating (or instructing their union organisers to negotiate) provision for union meetings to be held at the work place during working hours; this is in fact quite a standard union demand. Some extra determination may be needed from us to make sure that this becomes priority. Recent experience has shown that work place meetings could be the key to involving women in trade union matters.

There are some powerful weapons available to us in changing the way trade unions work. Perhaps the most important is our capacity for strong solidarity and co-operation in the face of difficulties, particularly among women in manual work who have shown great strength in facing up to men in management and, on occasion, in positions of trade union responsibility. Groups of women such as those in clerical and secretarial jobs, which have until now been largely unorganised, are gaining a powerful incentive to take action in the face of threatened redundancies.

One interesting possibility is to organise separately from the mainstream trade unions, a prospect that seems to have an immediate effect on them. The unions in the Netherlands, for example, have had to rethink their hostility to part-timers after the local post office union and local management at Groningen agreed in 1980 to a new work-scheme that wiped out half of the part-time jobs: those involved organised themselves into what was effectively a rival union of part-timers, picketed the post office building and forced the Government to intervene. The official union made a sudden U-turn in policy and now supports the demonstrators, all of whom have been reinstated.

In Britain, there have been many women's committees set up in various work places which may involve the members of any of the unions represented there, and sometimes women who are not members of any union. NALGO and NUPE in the public sector are beginning to develop the idea of women's committees operating within the union branch. Where this excludes many of the women working there, however, it may be preferable to work outside the union structure: at Thames TV, for example, a successful committee has started to operate in which any woman employed by the company is eligible to take part. At the United Nations in New York, I was involved in the Ad Hoc Women's Committee which was quite separate from the Staff Association, and although formally linked with it provided a powerful critique of its approach to management. There are many large establishments where a women's committee that is independent of union direction can have a strong impact.

Women organising within the trade union movement can make important breakthroughs. At the 1983 Conference of the Transport and General Workers' Union, a group of women achieved the rare feat of mobilising the delegates in opposition to the platform. They voted down a compromise statement and committed the whole union to a strong programme of positive action for the union's women members.

It is always worth recalling the early history of women's trade unionism in the face of all-male unions that simply excluded them from membership: they organised their own. When the ban on women members was lifted by the general unions after the First World War, the thriving women's unions were amalgamated with them. Women's participation in the trade union movement as a whole virtually collapsed as a result. The militant National Federation of Women Workers amalgamated with the National Union of General Workers (now the TGWU) in 1920, and the number of women officials involved fell rapidly from 16 to one. Women members of trade unions fell from 191,000 in 1918 to only 43,000 in 1923. During the whole of the 1920s and 1930s, with the worst depression ever known and the catastrophic decline of industries such as textiles where many women were employed, there was little effective organisation of working women. Now, with rising unemployment which is worst among women – although, as previously noted, largely unrecorded – there is a desperate need to learn the lessons of past failures, and to consolidate women's gains through the organisation of women by women in the trade unions.

The ghettoes of women's employment form a trap from which we have to escape. We need training and organisation to get into the major sectors of the economy which the trade unions and management together have kept as a male preserve. We need an end to any restrictions to part-time work, including the refusal of some unions to accept part-time members. We need positive action – in the face of male hostility – throughout the education and training system, in all places of employment, in all government departments and in the unions themselves. We need vastly increased facilities for child care and centres for other dependent relatives who need constant care. We need much greater involvement from all men in these issues. It all adds up to a social revolution.

Resources

Hear This, Brother: Women workers and union power, by Anna Coote and Peter Kellner, NS Report 1 (*New Statesman*, London, 1981) contains excellent material including a full discussion of women's attitudes and an introductory bibliography.

NALGO, *Equal Rights Working Party Report* (obtainable from 1 Mabledon Place, London, WC1) was first published in 1975 and is an early example of a union's commitment to positive action. Several other unions, especially the white-collar ones, now have their own publications on women's rights at work.

Many trade unions have made some attempts at positive action to fight discrimination against women, and a very useful survey of their efforts appears in chapter 4 of Sadie Robarts' *Positive Action for Women: The next step* (NCCL, 1981) available at £2 (for address see p. 17).

The early history of women in trade unions, and the processes absorbing them into the male unions between the wars, is boringly but usefully collected together in Norbert C. Soldon's *Women in British Trade Unions, 1874-1976* (Gill & Macmillan, Dublin, 1978).

An activist approach is taken by Jenny Beale in *Getting It Together: Women as trade unionists* (Pluto Press, London, 1983). The same publisher has also produced Cynthia Cockburn's *Brothers: Male dominance and technological change* (1983).

There is a new organisation of part-time workers organised by Brenda Clarke, 21 Ensdon Grove, Kingstanding, Birmingham.

3

Give and Take: Social Security and Tax

The systems of social security and personal taxation are two sides of the redistribution coin. They are the main ways of levelling out the differences between rich and poor, and eliminating the kind of desperate poverty of the Victorian age that we now see as 'Dickensian', part of fiction. The systems for redistributing income are especially important for women, who have always had much lower incomes than men and are less secure in terms of earning capacity in the future. As a reserve source of labour, we are last hired and first fired. For those whose financial security is a husband, there is the insecurity summed up in the American feminist slogan: 'Most women are only one man away from welfare'.

It is all the more serious, then, that the Sex Discrimination Act specifically excludes social security and tax, and that discrimination against women in fact lies at the heart of both systems. We can claim less than men from the State, and we are forced to pay out much more. Is this the way to justice and eventual equality? It is a mockery of any redistributive system that an already disadvantaged group should have special barriers placed in the way of getting a fair share.

The SS

Social security is a big issue for women, not only because of discrimination against us by the system but also because women, especially those with children, are the majority of all those living solely on benefits of one kind or another – sickness benefit, unemployment pay, supplementary benefit and the rest. Even more women are receiving partial benefits to supplement their low incomes, including child benefit and Family Income Supplement. Because of the very low levels of benefits available to women on SS, they and their children are becoming known as the 'new poor'.

It is astonishing that social security receives so little attention in the political arena. There is little mention of it in Parliament or in the political parties' debates. Less than 20 MPs were present at some of the most crucial stages of the Social Security No. 2 Bill in 1980, which made the first cuts in benefits for 50 years covering pensions, child benefits, sick pay and maternity allowance. These cuts were the result of the lively debate on social security taking place on the extreme right of the Conservative Party, where there are serious intentions of demolishing the 'Welfare State' either partially or completely. The alternative being proposed is 'the family', something seen through rose-coloured spectacles as the ideal way of supporting anybody who for whatever reason cannot earn their own living. The implications of this for women who are the mainstay of most families, and those with the least earning power or job security, would be devastating. The attacks on social security from the right wing are not being matched by a strong defence of it from the men of the left. It is pressure groups like the Child Poverty Action Group (CPAG) and the NCCL which are having to press the case for strengthening the system and raising the level of benefit, especially for women and their children. There is strong support also from women's organisations of almost all political convictions.

The Conservative Party has always been the least sympathetic towards social security claimants, who are often dismissed by better-off people as 'scroungers'. Even here, though, working with the women in the Party can prove to be an effective way of countering the strong pressure for cuts in the service. The CPAG has become expert at this, establishing itself as a widely-respected lobby which can consistently attract the most prominent Tory women – Lady Howe, Lady Soames, Baroness Young and others – to speak for them at Party conferences and elsewhere.

It was largely the Women's National Advisory Group of the Conservative Party that was instrumental in stopping many of the most savage cuts in social security proposed under the 1979-83 Thatcher government. In fact, the strength of what might be called the women's lobby in the Conservative Party, supported by some of the more enlightened men, is shown by the fact that although their pressure on social security was mainly defensive, to stop threatened cuts, they achieved a subsequent small rise in child benefits. The battle is never over inside the Tory Party, however: on 9 May 1983, just before the General Election was announced, there was a leak to the *Guardian* about high-level proposals to scrap child benefit altogether, providing a means-tested benefit instead. There was an immediate outcry and the proposals were quickly denied – no doubt after some strong words from women in the party about this sure vote-loser among women generally.

It is becoming widely accepted by many of the organisations in the 'poverty' field that the only measure that really benefits people in need is an increase in cash benefits. Provision for health, education, housing, public transport and other services, although they are very important to the poorest people, help the already better-off to a much greater extent. For any move towards greater economic equality in society, including equality between women and men, the most efficient and effective measure is the redistribution of the money. It is already a huge operation: in 1981, excluding the tax allowances, about £27,500 million was distributed to 22 million people in Britain. The numbers and amounts are growing as unemployment rises. Social security now accounts for 28 percent of public expenditure, twice as much as ten years ago (mainly because of rising unemployment) and double the size of any other government activity.

Women on SS

The social security system includes National Insurance benefits which are earnings-related and contributory, and those which are obtainable as of right by anybody in need, which are paid for by general taxation. The contributory benefits are obviously most useful to those in well-paid jobs, which continue for a long period and enable the employee to build up entitlement to a good level of benefits. Until very recently, married women usually paid lower levels of national insurance, and so had fewer benefits in their own right. For women the bottom line is the benefits which are non-contributory. Some, such as child benefit, are universal; others are means-tested, notably the supplementary benefit on which so many women with no other resources have to rely. Over 60 percent of SB recipients are women.

These millions of women are the worst-off in the country. There has been much discussion of exactly what 'poverty' is, and whether SB keeps people at or below this level. Perhaps the best definition is in the 1978 Report of the Supplementary Benefits Commission to Parliament:

To keep out of poverty people must have *an income which*

enables them to participate in the life of the community. They must be able, for example, to keep themselves reasonably fed, and well enough dressed to maintain their self-respect and to attend interviews for jobs with confidence. Their homes must be reasonably warm; their children should not feel ashamed by the quality of their clothing; the family must be able to visit relatives and give them something on their birthdays and at Christmas time; they must be able to read newspapers, and retain their television sets and their membership of trade unions and churches. And they must be able to live in a way which ensures, so far as possible, that public officials, doctors, teachers, landlords and others treat them with the courtesy due to every member of the community.

It is very clear from a CPAG survey of single parents, disabled and long-term unemployed people that the levels of supplementary benefit are much too low to allow this kind of participation in the community, and most of those surveyed were isolated or set apart by their poverty. They were cold, not eating well, often ill, badly dressed in cast-offs, unable to get around, and vulnerable to the smallest crisis, for example they could not afford the bus fare to a hospital. Many could not afford basic cleaning materials or toothpaste. They could not send their children on school visits, or buy the extra text books that many schools now require. The families were often going without essentials to pay the bills, having their household furniture repossessed or their gas and electricity cut off. They were often dumped in 'sink estates' miles from anywhere, where there was a sense of hopelessness, and the constant movement out of the area by anyone who could destroyed any sense of community that might otherwise have developed. Many of the women spoke of being 'trapped' in the house because they had no money for bus fares, or for buying anything in the shop. They suffered severely from depression and anxiety. Passing a shop window with nice new clothes or food could make them feel physically sick. Their aspirations were reduced to a good dinner, a trip to the zoo with the children or a night out – none of which was possible on the incomes they were struggling to live on.

Perhaps the worst miscalculation of the minimum amount needed to keep people fit and well is the rate for dependent children, and it is this which drags down any family which is surviving on supplementary benefits – mainly the single-parent families headed by women. The rates for children have been shown to be completely inadequate to keep them fed and clothed, and there is no allowance at all for the extra space they need, extra heating or all the other expenses of having children. A woman with these responsibilities can provide for children only by cutting down on her own food, clothing and transport, and isolating herself still further from ordinary life. A series of studies have shown that it is indeed the families with children that suffer the greatest hardship on SB.

The situation is now critical, since Conservative cuts in the value of benefits in the early 1980s, combined with inflation, left almost every group of claimants worse off in 1982 than at any time in the previous ten years; the total loss amounting to £2,000 million. In addition, the introduction of a new system of housing benefit which pays the rent direct to local authorities has wiped out one of the commonest survival strategies of families in crisis, which was to use the rent money for something else. There are now almost no ways of finding ready money to pay fuel bills, which results in long periods of disconnection during which the family suffers from severe cold, children cannot be kept occupied with homework or television, there is severe stress on everybody concerned, and an alarming rise in the rate of accidents, especially to children. Small babies can easily develop hypothermia, and cold houses are held largely responsible for the dramatic rise in baby deaths in the winter months, as well as the many more such deaths among old people.

To add insult to injury, people on long-term supplementary benefits are the target of constant attacks by many politicians as 'scroungers', and there are continual allegations made that many claimants are making false declarations. So great is the pressure on claimants, with the large numbers of DHSS investigators employed to detect any possible fraud, that some commentators have seen the system as being run as a means of discouraging people from claiming what they are legally entitled to. Almost no effort is made to advertise particular benefits which are not being claimed, or even to inform people of what they can claim at the time of their interview. In fact the interview itself is a humiliating and undermining experience for many people. A huge amount of benefit, estimated at about £400 million a year in 1979, is remaining unclaimed because of the lack of information, the intimidation of claimants, or a combination of the two.

It is especially alarming that 'fraud investigators' are allowed to penalise people by withdrawing the benefits on which they live, on the flimsiest of evidence that would be thrown out of court if there were a prosecution. Special attention is paid to single mothers, who according to the official guidelines are subject to 'discreet inquiries of employers, business associates or neighbours or, if time allows, approved special investigation methods such as observation, shadowing, liaison with police and checking of vehicle numbers'. The objective is to discover whether the woman has any relationship with a man, which would justify cutting off her benefits. The use of such measures, using 1,000 officials to track down what could be about £50 million of unjustified claims to social security, is grossly excessive in relation to any effort to publicise the *unclaimed* benefit which is eight times that amount. It also looks quite ludicrous in comparison with the small handful of staff attempting to deal with the real fraud in the financial system: tax and VAT payments which are concealed in the undeclared 'black' economy and which are worth an estimated £4,000 million. Tax fraud is *eighty times* as costly as the social security fraud which is used to justify harassment of women. The tax evaders are costing every legitimate taxpayer in the region of £160 a year, or over £3 a week. It is a strictly political decision to harass those on the bottom of the heap whilst turning a blind eye to those at the top.

Just in case life at the bottom is not hard enough for everyone concerned, the system has produced some special refinements for women only. The first of these, and the main basis for harassment of single mothers on SS, is the 'cohabitation rule'. The DHSS argues that a woman who lives with a man must be assumed to be getting money from him if she has no income of her own, although the law offers no means by which the woman can obtain any money from him. The same payments are considered to be taking place in the case of her children – regardless of the relationship, or lack of it, between them and the man in question. At the same time, the Inland Revenue will refuse the man any tax relief on his income for money which he actually pays to the woman and her children, since this department of Government rejects the principle of dependence between cohabitants who are not married to each other. There is great injustice being done to many people by this disagreement between government departments about the assumptions they make, and some people are left destitute as a result. All women should be entitled to a bare subsistence income, on the same basis as men. If the Government wishes to assume that men pay women they are living with, they would have to legislate to allow the woman to claim this money, although one can imagine great controversy if this were suggested. If the DHSS wanted to withdraw a woman's benefit on the grounds that she was getting this money, then the burden of proof should be on them in accordance with the basic principle of British justice that a person is deemed innocent until proved guilty in a court of law. If the man does in fact provide financial support, he should be given the incentive for declaring this to the authorities in the form of a tax return on which he could claim relief for the support of dependants. But how much simpler, and fairer, to reform the system by paying benefit without discrimination between women and men.

The operation of the 'cohabitation rule' is even worse in practice than the withdrawal of benefit from women and children who are really living with a man in some kind of joint household. The objective of the DHSS's spying on women is to establish whether *any* man is visiting their home, or appears to have any links with them at all, and the merest suspicion of this can be used to withdraw benefits. It frequently happens that visits by male relatives are misinterpreted by the SS investigators, and the presence of male lodgers, flat-mates or friends can have the same effect. All of this places an intense strain on a woman's attempts to live a normal life, including the presence of men, and the children are easily disturbed by the tensions involved. The 'cohabitation rule' is probably the meanest and most spiteful aspect of the social security system, targeted at the most vulnerable women and children. The discrimination against women which lies behind it should be a prime target for anyone committed to basic justice.

A challenge has been mounted to the discrimination against women in Britain's social security system, from the unlikely quarter of the EEC. The European Court has directed the British Government to change the law so as to make it the same for women and men claiming certain benefits. One of the top EEC priorities for reform is the system which penalises two-parent families that rely mainly or entirely on the mother's income: she is unable to claim sickness benefits for her dependants, for example, when she is ill. The same has also been applied to family income supplement, supplementary benefit, unemployment benefit and other payments. The only exception has been where the husband is physically or mentally disabled, a condition which does not apply to the wife when the husband is the main income-earner. This is now being slowly revised to make it possible for families to nominate the 'head of household' who is to receive the benefit for dependants.

While conceding that a certain number of two-parent families with an unemployed, low-paid or disabled husband can now be treated more fairly, the DHSS seems to be fighting a rearguard action to protect some blatantly unjust rules in other cases, and even to invent new ones which will adversely affect women in the greatest difficulty. This particularly applies to those with disabilities, or who are caring for people in this position. The invalid care allowance, paid to people who stay at home to care for a severely disabled relative, is not given to women if they are married or living with a man. These are the great majority of women involved in exclusive, full-time care, often for more than one dependent person at a time and in many cases their husbands' relatives rather than their own. At the same time, married women who are themselves disabled are forced to undergo a special 'housework test' which is an official form, normally interpreted so harshly that women are routinely refused the disability pension that is automatically available for all men, and single women, who are at the same level of disability. Women's loss of earnings at the onset of a serious illness or injuries are automatically disregarded if they are married. The majority of those applying have not in fact been the full-time 'housewives' they are officially described as. The bitterness of women who suffer this discrimination, as a bar to obtaining either a disability pension or the invalid care allowance, became evident when the EOC advertised in four women's magazines on the subject in 1981. Over 10,000 letters of complaint were received within a few weeks, and the EOC reported: 'A striking factor was the repeated expressions of simple gratitude from correspondents who had felt themselves to be worthless and forgotten.'

Keeping a good woman down

The latest turn of the discrimination screw, perhaps to compensate for the easing up on two-parent families with the mother as breadwinner, is the new rule applying to unemployment benefit for women who lose their jobs. This was introduced with lightning speed after the publication of the Rayner Report in 1982, in contrast to the snail's pace at which the removal of existing discrimination is moving. The rule is that all mothers, and the fairly small number of single fathers, will be ineligible for unemployment benefit even if they have paid the necessary

National Insurance premiums, unless they can prove that they already have someone to look after the children. Since unemployed parents will not be able to pay a child-minder, they will not be able to prove that they *already* have one, even if they can show that someone is available as soon as they get a job and an income. The official verdict in such cases is that the women are 'unavailable for work' and therefore denied the dole for which they have been making contributions. This money might have made it financially possible to get a child-minder, for at least short periods of time, in order to search for work and attend interviews. The rule is the most effective possible trap for all women with children, whether they have just been made redundant or are trying to get a paid job after full-time work in the house.

Once in the trap it is becoming increasingly harder to climb out, especially for women. If we have children, we will be denied unemployment benefit to which we have contributed. Part-time or informal work, which for many of us could be the gradual way out of the vicious circle, is savagely penalised by the benefit regulations, based on the view of claimants as 'scroungers': they simply withdraw the same amount of benefit as you are earning, apart from a small amount which will probably be needed for fares and meals out. Low-paid jobs are also taxed so heavily, and benefits withdrawn at such low income levels, that increasing numbers of women are being forced to stay on the State benefits for the sake of the free school meals, children's clothing, rent and other allowances. This is the infamous 'poverty trap', which particularly affects women and children. The dilemma is especially difficult for single mothers or women married to low-paid or unemployed husbands, since the only jobs available to them are so low-paid that they cannot provide an escape from the trap.

One social security benefit, more than any other, holds the key to releasing women from the poverty trap. This is the child benefit which is paid across the board to all mothers for their children, unless they are on social security. In its earlier form as the family allowance, or 'women's wage', this payment was the direct descendant of one of the earliest and most radical demands of the women's suffrage movement. It was in the early 1900s that Eleanor Rathbone, Secretary of the Liverpool Suffrage Society, worked out a scheme for a guaranteed weekly allowance for mothers, and with other radical suffragists from Lancashire and Cheshire she campaigned for it within the early Labour Party, in the women's textile unions, and later as an independent MP. In the 1920s

41

Eleanor wrote a book, *The Disinherited Family: a plea for the endowment of the family*, arguing that the 'family wage' did not take into account the number of children in a family or whether the father was actually sharing his wages with them. Her solution was to provide a regular payment to mothers to feed and clothe their children. The family allowance was introduced as one of the first reforming measures of the 1945 Labour Government, and despite repeated difficulties and the inadequate levels of payment, the basic principle has survived – so far.

In 1976, soon after the sacking of the only woman in the Labour Cabinet – Barbara Castle – the Government prepared to abandon its Manifesto commitment to a new child allowance for mothers, arguing that it would cost too much and would be opposed by the men. Fortunately, a civil servant was bold enough to leak the information to the Child Poverty Action Group. Publication of the plans, followed by a storm of protest from women, forced a complete about-turn thus ensuring relatively good levels of new child benefit, payable for virtually all children except those on SS, and paid directly to their mothers unless a specific alternative had been authorised by her. Since then, however, the value of the benefit has declined. Even after a rise in child benefit in the 1983 Budget, support for families with children was still less than in the 1950s. The decline has hit particularly hard at families in the 'poverty trap' and at women with children and an employed husband who is not contributing adequately to their support. There is a surprising number of families in this kind of hidden poverty trap, just as Eleanor Rathbone described in her original explanation for her scheme; some of the women involved have nothing except child benefit to live on.

At the lowest levels, families on supplementary benefit, the falling child benefit paid to other families has led to a corresponding cut in the SS payments for children, in the attempt to provide an 'incentive' to seek paid work. It has been argued by the CPAG and others that the levels of child benefit are the crucial determinant of the sub-poverty levels for families on SB, as well as of the safety net for those who are not sharing in the father's income: they therefore provide some kind of a floor level for the pay that women have to get before they can improve their families' income by getting a job. All low-income people, whether wage-earners or not, should benefit from a realistic level of child benefit. Children would of course be the greatest beneficiaries. If we consider also the effect of the maternity allowance and grant, benefits paid to women which have fallen catastrophically in value over the last ten or fifteen years, it is clear that the guarantee of our babies' and children's health and welfare, as well as our own, must lie in raising the cash benefits paid to women.

Where is the money to come from?

Tax

The tax system is the direct reverse of social security: instead of distributing resources by cash payments, it levels income by a graduated scale of deductions from earnings. However, it also offers a range of personal allowances which increase the recipient's income just as effectively as a cash allowance. It may come as no surprise to find that the tax allowances, of all kinds, are much more favourable to men, despite their already higher income, than to women. Those who would like to see a fairer system of redistribution argue strongly that the two systems of social security and tax must be dealt with together. Increased payments of child benefit, maternity grant, and all other social security payments should be funded from a reduction in the special tax allowances now given either mainly or exclusively to men. The biggest prize of all, needless to say, is the biggest allowance of them all apart from the standard single person's allowance: the married man's tax allowance.

The total value of the married man's allowance is about £3,000 million. During extensive consultations carried out by the Inland Revenue about reform of the system, virtually every organisation expressing an opinion has come out in favour of abolishing this unfair give-away to men; they include the women's sections of all the major political parties. The only real difference of opinion was over the best way to redistribute the money to give a fair deal to women. A clear majority supported the idea of using the entire saving to give a large increase in child benefit, and to link it to an index of average earnings so that its value is not allowed to fall later. This does indeed make sense in tax terms, since child benefit has replaced not only the family allowance, but also the old tax allowances for children which were previously given to fathers. The married man's allowance itself can only be justified at all on the basis that some married men are supporting others with their incomes, especially children. The change would simply ensure that the benefit was provided where this was actually the case, in direct proportion to the number of children being supported. Since the money is paid to the mother except where specifically authorised by her, the child benefit would directly help the women who are working at home to take care of the children. It would also make sense to supplement the child benefit by increasing the invalid care allowance and making sure that all the women looking after dependent relatives were receiving it.

Fundamental reform of the tax system to eliminate discrimination between women and men, particularly those who are married, is long overdue. Any party that seriously wants the women's vote will have to show that it means business here. There is no mistaking the strength of feeling. There was a campaign against discrimination in tax in 1977 and 1978 which involved the EOC, *Woman's Own* magazine and the *Sunday Times*, which brought in a flood of letters from women demanding an end to our overpayments of tax. It was as a direct result of this pressure that the Labour Government announced some changes to the tax system in 1978. The Inland Revenue for the first time condescended to reply directly to women about our incomes and tax affairs. A woman paying income tax now receives her own tax rebate (unless she is self-employed, her income is unearned or she and her husband are assessed at a rate of tax above the basic rate, in which case her payments still go to him). A few small allowances for men only were stopped. However, no basic change has been made: a husband is still expected to declare his wife's income as part of his own, and to take responsibility for the tax on it. The only way out is for both of them to opt for separate assessment, which means their allowances are much lower unless they are in an exceptionally high tax bracket.

Pressure for change is mounting, although the Conservative Government has been resisting strongly, particularly in the all-male Family Policy Group which has taken over important Cabinet functions. The Chancellor of the day, Sir Geoffrey Howe, received overwhelming support for his Green Paper on reforming the tax system and in 1983 decided to scrap the married man's allowance for the benefit of children and of women working at home. The Family Policy Group overwhelmed him and vetoed any change: instead, the married man's allowance was actually increased. There has been a storm of protest from women's organisations including those in the Conservative Party, who pointed out that the Labour and SDP parties were now committed to a fairer distribution of the allowances. An unidentified Conservative woman told the *Guardian*, which had broken the story, 'The women's section are united in wanting independent taxation. We now account for 60 percent of the membership of the party . . .' Obviously we have not heard the last of this particular battle.

It is in fact crucial to the debate on equality in society: equal gross pay, because of discrimination in tax, is converted into much lower take-home pay. At the basic rate of tax, a woman who is married will take home about £5 a week less than a married man doing the same job. Where part of a couple's joint income attracts a higher rate of tax, it is the husband who is allowed the basic rate first, while part of the wife's income – even though it is probably lower – is taxed at the higher rate, making for a very large loss in take-home pay. Husbands are also entitled to other forms of tax relief not applied to women's pay packets, such as the full allowance for interest on a joint mortgage to which both partners are contributing. Our earnings are effectively being stolen by the Inland Revenue: we are being robbed.

We should also be much more aware of the tax allowances being given away in our name to a group of very highly-paid people, almost all of them men, even though they are not defined as men's allowances in so many words. It should be a matter of interest to us that companies are starting to pay their executives and even middle-ranking employees in cars, houses, private health insurance, private schooling for their children and even expensive clothes, in order to avoid the tax which would have been paid out if these men had received the cash and bought their own. By far the biggest give-away by the Inland Revenue to the higher-paid is the company car system. About two-thirds of all new cars are in fact being bought by companies, mainly to distribute to middle-grade and senior employees as part of their pay-packets and with little relevance to the job they do. Quite apart from the distortions of transport policy that arise out of the enormous tax subsidies for company cars, the system results in a shift of tax allowances to the better-off, mainly male, taxpayers at the expense of everyone else.

Women who have no income of their own are also getting a very raw deal from the tax system, which should be acknowledging their work, especially in taking care of dependent children and other relatives. They are receiving very low child benefit; most of them are excluded from the invalid care allowance; their right to the married allowance given to their husbands is non-existent; and they can be kept in ignorance of tax returns made in their name. To add insult to injury, they suffer great distress from the Inland

Revenue's treatment of their small personal savings, often achieved at great personal cost by economising on the housekeeping or on the money for their own clothes and other needs. For many such women their only personal resource is a small building society or post office account which they keep under their own control to spend on presents or personal needs, or save for emergencies. The tax system ruthlessly exposes the exact details of the woman's savings to her husband, without any reference to her, and taxes him accordingly. Needless to say his personal savings are not made known to her in this way, nor is his income. The injustice of this leads to a great deal of friction and unhappiness in some marriages. An immediate reform to help women in this position would be to set a fixed allowance for the personal savings of each marriage partner, particularly the one with no earned income, which should be exempt from any interference from the tax authorities. If tax officials disclose her savings to her husband, then they must also do the same with his finances – the simplest way being to require her signature on all joint tax returns and correspondence. It would not cost a penny, or require any changes in procedure. The fact that this simple measure has not been introduced probably indicates that the excuses from governments about the difficulty of implementing a fairer tax system are little more than a smoke-screen to hide the political bias in favour of men in the whole system of public finance.

There are organisations, particularly those concerned with older women who are financially dependent on their husbands, which argue that women should have a personal tax allowance that they could transfer partly or totally to their husband's pay. This could be of direct benefit to the women concerned only if it also ensures their rights to full disclosure of the joint tax return, and to a fair share of the after-tax earnings in cases where this is not taking place. The whole question of whether married women with no paid job but a well-paid husband should have a transferable allowance is a highly political one between the left and right. Their claims have to be set against the very urgent need for relief on the part of women with low incomes, and those with small children or elderly and disabled relatives to look after. There is a strong case for channelling the money that could be freed in abolishing the allowance for married men into the payment of cash benefits to the people, mainly women, who are in most need of help to support others.

The majority of us are paying far more than our fair share of tax, which has been going up much faster for many women than the much-publicised local rates. At the same time, we are being denied our share of the cash benefits provided through the social security system. Families with children, in particular, are becoming rapidly worse off because of the combined effects of cuts in child benefit and social security and the increases in taxation. Between the tax year 1960-61 and that of 1982-83, tax on average earnings has gone up by three-quarters for single people, doubled for married couples (although much more for the wife than the husband), quadrupled for couples with two children and increased by eight times for those with four. Taxation is harshest at the lowest levels, with almost all the families whose earnings had to be topped up by family income supplement now having money deducted from it for tax. A family with three children could be taxed so heavily that it is worse off on earnings of £110 a week, than on less than £80, because of the simultaneous withdrawal of benefits. The system is becoming indescribably mean towards those in most need of financial help. Instead of redistributing some income from the better-off to those with least resources and most responsibilities, the flow is going the other way. The first act of the Conservative Government after being re-elected in 1983 was to cut taxes for the well off, and to make further cuts in benefits for the poor.

The unfairness between rich and poor, wage-earners and those working for nothing, and men and women is increasing. At the same time, money is spent on harassing the low-paid for any suspicion of 'scrounging' while the blatant tax evasion by big companies and wealthy individuals is virtually ignored. Both social security and tax, as the twin levers of a mechanism to redistribute income, should be subjected to a complete overhaul. Women have already shown great resentment at the injustices of our tax system and cash benefits. It is time our claims for financial justice were taken seriously by the politicians of all parties.

Resources

Two organisations which are publishing and campaigning for greater equality in social security and tax are the NCCL (for address see p. 17) and the CPAG (1 Macklin Street, London WC2).

A comprehensive guide to the social security benefits available, who is entitled to them and how you should claim is the *National Welfare Benefits Handbook*, edited by Jo Tunnard and Nicholas

Warren, price £1, available from CPAG. There are regular new editions to update the information. The CPAG's survey of claimants is published as *Living from Hand to Mouth*, price £1.20.

Ruth Lister and Leo Wilson have written in detail on two-parent families dependent on the woman's income, in *The Unequal Breadwinner: a new perspective on women and social security* (NCCL, 1976), price 35p.

A useful survey of all aspects of disability for women is Jo Campling's *Better Lives for Disabled Women* (Virago, London, 1979), available at £1.25.

There are two useful pamphlets on taxation: *Income Tax and Sex Discrimination* by Patricia Hewitt (NCCL, 1979) available at 85p, and *The Poverty of Taxation*, on the crippling taxation of the low-paid (CPAG, 1982), price £1.75.

A comprehensive summary of the workings of social security and tax is in chapter 3 of *Women's Rights: A practical guide*, by Anna Coote and Tess Gill (Penguin, London, Third edition, 1981, see p. 142).

48

4

Sickness and Health

Women's health has always been a vital element in women's campaigns for a better deal, and it has been one of the leading feminist issues. The focus has been on health problems affecting women only: our treatment by the mainly male specialists in obstetrics and gynaecology, the whole framework of treatment in pregnancy and childbirth, and issues of reproduction in general. The real political hot potatoes, of course, have been questions about women's fertility: first contraception, later abortion, and all the time a struggle for safer and better provision for antenatal care and birth itself.

Margaret Sanger and other women were pioneers in setting up family planning clinics in the teeth of 'respectable' opposition and ridicule. The new clinics provided life-saving fertility control for millions of women during the Depression of the 1930s and afterwards. Although we now have the right to free family planning for all in the NHS, there still remains a need for political pressure from women to make facilities available to everybody. Recent cuts in the health service have involved the closure of family planning clinics, so that many women are forced to go to GPs who often have no training in fitting diaphragms and coils, for example, thus limiting the choice of method and also the friendly counselling that is often supplied in the specialist clinics. There are also many issues to be resolved about the use of new contraceptives without proper knowledge of their side-effects, and the availability of sterilisation. While many women and men find it hard or even impossible to get a sterilisation in the NHS on request, other women are being sterilised without their informed consent, often at a time of greatest stress such as immediately after the birth of a child. It is important that sterilisation should be available, together with counselling if required, to those who decide for themselves that this is the best form of contraception; it should never be imposed by others.

Every contraceptive failure, where the couple concerned does not intend to have a baby, means that abortion will come into question. This is always a very difficult choice for women. It is always better to avoid the need for an abortion if at all possible, and women do not choose it lightly – despite the propaganda from the opposition who try to present it as something undertaken frivolously. Many of the men who make pompous statements about it, whether in Parliament or in the pubs, treat it in the most simplistic and crude way, with little thought about the implications of bearing an unwanted child both for the woman and for the child. They pay little attention to the responsibilities of the father – indeed, there is almost no thought of increasing the pressure on men to look after unwanted children for whom they are responsible. There is even less thought given to improving the provision of child-care facilities or a realistic child benefit that would allow a woman to share the burden of rearing a child with those other members of society who may seek to force her into unwanted childbirth. The debate among the men is riddled with hypocrisy about children and about the responsibilities of women and men. No wonder, then, that women have become more and more determined to resolve by ourselves the question of whether or not to carry a foetus to term.

Abortion has always been an important means of limiting the number of births. We are very fortunate to be able to use relatively efficient contraceptive measures to prevent many of the abortions that would otherwise take place, and we are also lucky to have the technology to ensure safe abortions and early detection of pregnancy to allow them to be done at an early stage. Without legal provision for abortion, women would be forced into the hands of profiteers charging exorbitant fees, and subject to no safeguards. Making abortion illegal is a guarantee that many women will suffer excruciating pain, and some will die. Others, unable to get an abortion they want, will be forced into childbirth and have a child as 'punishment' for their crimes – as the old moralists used to insist. This is a sure recipe for much unhappiness, child abuse and the disruption of the 'family' unit forcibly created in this way.

A whole series of Bills have been introduced in Parliament since the passage of the 1967 Abortion Act, which seek to turn the clock back to the days of illegal abortion. What is perhaps most striking, as one MP told me, is the growing opposition from women to these attempts by men to change a law which is so vitally important to us. Enormous controversy is stirred up by each attempt, but the flood of mail has changed since the passage of the 1967 Act, from a 50-50 split for and against abortion to a 90 percent majority for it by the time of the Corrie Bill of 1979. Overwhelmingly, women wrote to their MPs to express horror at the idea of returning to the bad old days of illegal abortion. The slogan 'A woman's right to choose' is increasingly the theme of women's demands of their male 'representatives'. It was certainly this opposition from women that turned around many of the men who until then had claimed abortion as exclusively a matter for their own male conscience.

What should be the happier side of our fertility, bearing a child who is wanted, has also been the subject of much distress among women. There has been steady campaigning over many years for less of the unwanted medical intervention and greater control by the woman herself over the birth. Women have always known about the connection between a positive experience of birth and their subsequent relationship with the child, but far too many doctors persist in treating it as an isolated event, and the mother's feelings as of no importance. Antenatal procedures treat women as little more than containers for the almighty foetus. The National Childbirth Trust, an organisation mainly of women who teach techniques for a woman to control her own labour, has never been given recognition in the NHS as part of antenatal provision. There is enormous resistance by the doctors to women's right to give birth at home with a midwife, although there is no evidence that hospitals are safer. Women in labour are often left alone in hospitals at times of great stress and pain. There has had to be a struggle by women to have the father or a friend present and involved at the birth. Many women are subjected to procedures and drugs without their full knowledge and consent, the most common being induction of the birth to speed it up at times convenient to the doctors, which is very distressing and painful for the woman involved. A national survey by *Parents* magazine in 1981 showed that a third of the women giving birth had their labour induced, almost two-thirds were given drugs without their consent and 37 percent had serious complaints about the hospital's treatment of the birth.

Not only do women suffer unnecessarily, but some of the medical procedures are likely to be harmful to the child being born. Many permanent handicaps are the result of damage at the time of birth, including brain damage. The resources spent on elaborate monitoring and other unnecessary interventions, whose effects are not very well studied, would be far better spent on life-saving equipment and incubators for all babies at risk immediately after birth. Many children could be spared permanent damage in this way, and the numbers of parents who face life-long difficulties of caring for a handicapped daughter or son would be reduced – surely one of the top priorities for any national health service.

It is vitally important also that we recognise the economic factor in the hazards of pregnancy and childbirth. Working-class mothers are now twice as likely as middle-class women to suffer the death of their baby at birth or within the first month, and four or five times as likely to see them die in their first year of life. This is almost certainly the result of the women's poor diet, bad housing and working conditions marked by pollution, damp and cold, and a lifetime of lower general standards of health. An adequate maternity grant for all women is absolutely essential as the first step to preventing many unnecessary deaths and handicapped babies, and to ensuring that all our children have a fair chance of health from the start. The level of maternity grant is a joke at the moment, and is not even paid to many women with the worst problems. The men who are the policy-makers often give lip-service to the importance of maternal and child health, but when it comes to practical measures they show their lack of concern by neglecting even the simplest reforms proposed time and again by women's pressure groups, voluntary organisations such as the Spastics Society, and the Government's own reports.

The problems relating to our own fertility have been perhaps the biggest issue for women for at least a 100 years, and the battle is still raging around abortion and women's control over childbirth. It is important, though, that we should not see health issues only in these terms: we are whole people, with health issues relating to our whole bodies as well as our mental well-being, and we should be concerned about all health issues in the broadest sense. For better health we need decent jobs, better transport, personal safety, less stress in personal relationships and in the whole of our lives, more rest and recreation, better housing, child-care services – in fact a whole range of changes in how resources are allocated towards us and our needs. These changes depend on our being effectively organised and politically and personally more powerful than we are now. Being organised is in fact an essential element in our own well-being. Many women at the moment feel powerless, overworked, trapped in situations they did not want, insecure, isolated, fearful, and above all – depressed. Physical and mental energy come from feeling in control of your life, having real choices and being involved with others to find ways of organising for a change for the better.

The National Health

Women depend heavily on the National Health Service, even more than men. There are very few women who could afford to pay for private treatment if they became ill or had an accident. We are much more likely than men to be out of the job market through unemployment or retirement, which automatically excludes us from the health insurance schemes which are provided as a fringe benefit for some better-paid employees. We depend more than men on the NHS for doctors' visits, hospital services, prescription medicines, dental care and all the rest of its services. In fact, women use *all* health services more than men do, for our own health problems, quite apart from our responsibility for the health of children, and elderly or disabled relatives. We have a special need for the maternal and child health services and the family planning facilities, since it is almost always women who have to take responsibility for contraception. The majority of mental patients are women, because of the stresses and strains of our daily lives. Since we are survivors, though, women also make up the overwhelming majority of old people needing the geriatric services. Many of the health sectors serving large numbers of women are under-funded, with mental health and geriatric specialities being the 'Cinderella services' of the NHS.

Meanest of all are the salaries and wages paid to the hundreds of thousands of women who keep the entire health service operating – as nurses and midwives, medical professionals including physiotherapists, dieticians and radiographers, and the large number of administrators, mainly at the lower levels, who actually deal with the patients.

The NHS is at the centre of the whole 'Welfare State', the jewel in the crown of the post-war Labour Government and one of its most important legacies to those who came after. Successive governments have grappled with the enormous problems of the NHS, added or subtracted charges for various bits and pieces, but been forced by public opinion to support at least the idea of free hospitals and GP services.

A 'Think Tank' report to the Conservative Government in 1982, which proposed what amounted to dismantling the NHS, raised such a storm of protest that Ministers disowned it almost as soon as it was mentioned. However, they remained busy promoting private medical insurance by all means possible, while closing down hospitals, family planning clinics and other services – some of them to re-open shortly afterwards as private facilities.

What is it about the NHS that makes it such a big political issue? Why should charges for false teeth or medicines be so fiercely debated? For the answer, we have to look at Britain before the NHS was started, or the many other countries which continue to rely on a system of private medicine backed by various insurance policies. Many people in Britain, especially the older women, remember only too well the pre-war fear of illness and high cost of medical treatment which left many people without proper care. In the United States today there are many millions of people who are outside any kind of medical insurance, especially the low-paid and the unemployed, and who cannot afford proper medical attention. Even those with private insurance, which is generally provided as a fringe benefit of their job, find if they are seriously ill or have a bad accident that the insurance runs out half-way through treatment, and they can easily be made bankrupt by the medical bills.

Because of the vital importance to us of the NHS, women need to become closely involved in the fight for more health resources, and at the same time in the many detailed decisions about its priorities which are having to be made virtually every day. The press and other media often distort the debate by sensational reports about the latest treatment for rare diseases, obscuring the problem of how to benefit the largest number of people facing common ailments whose treatment has been starved of essential funds. For example, can we really afford to develop a programme of heart transplants, which actually offer very little in the way of real lifesaving prospects? It makes no sense to divert funds to this while we close down maternity facilities and freeze the provision for treatment of small babies at risk of permanent disability or death from complications at birth. The NHS is becoming badly distorted, starving essential programmes in order to invest more and more money in new and often experimental machinery and drugs, which are being developed by the big medical companies at prices which are becoming prohibitive. It can quite easily happen that a powerful hospital consultant can order an expensive machine of unproven usefulness, such as a whole-body scanner, or even organise public fund-raising for the machine, obliging the NHS to divert revenue to operating and staffing it, when the same machine is available in another nearby hospital with plenty of spare capacity. At the same time, whole wards or even hospitals providing a valuable service to the community for a wide range of health problems may be closed down.

It is above all the preventive medicine which suffers from a decision-making process that favours the more sensational or prestigious aspects of medical care. Many patients who could benefit from advice on diet or general lifestyle, or who need help in giving up smoking or heavy drinking, are getting no help at all until the point where their health collapses and dramatic (and expensive) hospital treatment is required. The misery and sheer economic cost of people operating for long periods with chronic health problems that could be easily treated or alleviated by a change in lifestyle are an indication that NHS planners have been unable to get the balance of services right. On the one hand, there is too much emphasis on the use of medical technology for its own sake: some terminally ill patients are made to endure elaborate medical intervention which may achieve nothing except cause additional pain and distress, and women in labour are subjected to elaborate and expensive devices which may actually be dangerous for the child. On the other, life-saving casualty units are closed down, and people are kept waiting for months or years for simple operations. The senior consultants – usually male– who effectively control the system seem to be mainly interested in the glamour of an elaborate new treatment – constantly encouraged by the sales representatives of firms producing the experimental equipment and drugs. The great majority of patients, who need preventive health care or the tried, trusted and *safe* treatments, are of little interest to the consultants. Our lack of priority in their eyes is reflected in the artificial 'waiting lists', created, at least in part, by the refusal of surgeons – again usually male – to do enough operating sessions for routine conditions like varicose veins and hernias. This approach can be very profitable for the surgeons, since some better-off patients will 'go private' to jump the queue. Women suffer in large numbers from arthritis, rheumatism, varicose veins and problems of the uro-genital tract, and even where there are operations and other forms of treatment that could help they are often not receiving them. The bias of research also tends to be away from these disabling health problems that particularly afflict women, predominantly older women, who are of perhaps the least interest to the medical profession as a whole.

The system needs turning upside down to make it accountable to us as patients and to provide as a first priority the routine service needed by the greatest number. Community Health Councils representing our interests as patients should be given more powers, and elected representatives should run regional and district health authorities – not the political appointees, bureaucrats and consultants who are in charge of them at the moment. Making the health service more accountable will require a much better-informed public, aware of our own responsibility for maintaining reasonable health; a health and safety policy that will cut down accidents and environmental poisons; and an end to the kind of medical sensation whipped up by the press, which revolves around the most expensive machines and the most sophisticated new techniques. There is a very important place for new treatments, properly planned and evaluated; but they should never be allowed to snatch funds from preventive health programmes and community care for the huge numbers of elderly, disabled or mentally ill and those with routine conditions that are capable of straightforward treatment. The NHS was set up to care for all the people, not just the few who interest the consultants.

As women we need to change our attitude towards doctors, too, and especially to understand something they know only too well: that they have no answer, or the wrong answer, to some of the most common health complaints presented by women, day in and day out, at a GP's surgery. The epidemic of depression and chronic anxiety among so many married women, for example, is almost always answered with a prescription for tranquillisers and other drugs. These fail to resolve the original problem, often make it worse, and create problems of dependence and addiction which have now become serious health hazards in their own right. The same limit to doctors' powers to solve health problems is seen in other very common complaints, especially back problems, stomach pains, and many common women's complaints such as cystitis. Many honest GPs will admit that they are often helpless to do anything for these ailments except give pain-killing drugs or tranquillisers for temporary relief. But they are up against the popular myth that the doctor must have an answer, and our insistence on prescriptions for drugs as some kind of magical response to all our problems. Women even go to the doctor with personal or sexual problems, or perhaps advice on diet, convinced by the agony-columns in magazines and the press that this is the right thing to do. We fail to understand that many doctors are unable to cope with their own personal and sexual problems – let alone help patients with theirs – while their knowledge of nutrition is very poor. Doctors have a vital part to play in the health service, but they are not God despite the fact that the system treats them like Her. It is important for us to understand what they can and cannot do, and how the recruitment and training of doctors can be improved, as part of our better understanding and use of the whole health service.

Ordinary women, as users of the NHS and often as carers for sick people at home as well, would make very different kinds of decisions about priorities from those made by the present decision-makers. We would want to improve the pay and working conditions of health workers (mostly women) directly involved in the personal care and nursing of patients, rather than those of the highly-paid doctors. The latest and most expensive technology would be considered on its merits, not on the basis of massively expensive promotions and high-pressure sales techniques used at present to influence investment decisions. We would look very seriously at ways of saving some of the public money which is now being handed out to the drug companies. The Greenfield Report on the prescribing of drugs, published in 1982, suggested that millions of pounds a year could be saved by the simple change of allowing pharmacists to issue the cheapest brand of the drug prescribed, instead of the brand heavily promoted by advertising and costing from twice to nine times the amount. GPs in particular, since they are not experts on drugs, tend to remember the brand names from advertising on which the companies spend thousands of pounds for each GP in the country.

The report showed that out of the 4,000 branded drugs officially listed by the manufacturers, only about 30 could not be replaced in this way. The change would almost halve the drugs bill for GP prescriptions, thereby eliminating the need to charge people for essential ones. Alternatively it has been suggested that the savings, estimated by chemists' representatives at £170 million, would pay for restoring many of the recent cuts in health services, plus providing desperately needed life-saving equipment such as intensive care facilities for small babies at risk of permanent handicap or premature death. With such a choice it is virtually certain that ordinary people, and most health workers, would welcome big changes in drug use within the NHS, combining the switch to cheaper brands with a reduced use of dangerously addictive drugs such as tranquillisers and barbiturates, and a very rigorous approach to new machines and equipment that gives priority to those of proven life-saving value rather than as yet unproven diagnostic interest.

Improvements in the NHS are not just a question of how money is budgeted, important though that is. We have to review our overall priorities and bring the Cinderella services up to the standard of the more exciting and glamorous work, such as the exceptionally fine provision for serious injury and acute illness which the NHS provides, one which is possibly the best in the world. It is the routine services, the GPs and outpatient clinics which are in serious trouble. The problem is not just lack of money but also the planners' disregard for the patients as people. Absolute priority is given to the convenience of the highly-paid doctors at the expense of other health workers and the patients. There has been a rapid decline in the availability of GPs as they insist on an appointments system operating days in advance, with little or no reduction in the waiting times at some surgeries. Home visits have been restricted by many GPs, and emergency cover is all too often delegated to inadequate commercial services. It is virtually impossible to remove bad GPs once they are in place, even if they are themselves ill or alcoholic; and some inner-city areas suffer very badly from a shortage of doctors, exacerbated by an increase in private practice which leads to neglect of patients on the NHS list. Rural areas, too, are having local services cut back savagely. While 'community care' is the official policy, the reality is an increasing centralisation of services, taking them further from the community than ever.

In the hospitals, out-patients are often kept waiting for hours to see a doctor, despite a rigid appointments system, and there is particular abuse of women coming for antenatal check-ups. Patients are sometimes treated rudely or inconsiderately, with no real possibility of a complaint being heard. A hurried visit to the consultant fails to provide explanations about the problem, or advice on how to cope with it, which is what so many patients and their families need, especially if their problem is chronic or they have to have a major operation. Perhaps the most effective way of meeting such people's needs is to form groups of those suffering from the same illness or problem, for advice and mutual support – and this is a fairly simple task that could be easily done by an NHS less dedicated to the 'quick fix' approach of the consultants. The job of counselling people with health problems and disabilities is a

very important one for which people can be trained. It uses skills in communication which most doctors simply do not have, although many of the nurses and other women in the health service actually do a great deal of counselling, informally and without recognition.

The worst of the human problems in the NHS, especially in hospitals, usually arise out of the rigid hierarchy whereby doctors make all the decisions, and everybody else, even if they are better trained in the particular work involved, has to accept their authority without question. It is particularly bad for everyone concerned that there is a master-servant relationship between doctors and nurses. Highly-skilled nurses and other health professionals are not able to take conversion courses to lead to a doctor's qualification, although their background and experience would make them excellent doctors in many cases. New ideas arising in other medical specialities, from physiotherapy to nutrition, can be blocked because of the conservatism of the doctors. Even more serious for us is their resistance to any forms of treatment which they do not understand and which they dismiss as 'alternative' medicine, although osteopathy, chiropractice and other specialities have a better success record for certain ailments than the officially recognised ones. The effect of this exclusive attitude is to make a range of 'alternative' treatments available only to those who can afford to pay. It also means that there is no system for evaluating the many different forms of treatment for which claims are being made.

A positive health policy

It is often said, and with reason, that the NHS as it works now is on the verge of collapse. Not only is the service itself in a state of constant crisis with cuts in the services for which there is increasing need, but in fact the general state of health in this country has *not* improved since the NHS was founded. Some serious health problems, such as tuberculosis, and a number of serious children's illnesses, have been overcome – but others, including heart disease and cancer, have simply taken their place. There are many preventable injuries from accidents on the roads, in industry and at home. The proportion of people with a chronic disability has increased. The NHS is vitally important in treating the casualties of our unhealthy way of life, and we must defend and improve the service. But at the same time, much greater emphasis is needed on eliminating the known causes of sickness and injury, providing preventive health care and information that will help people to stay healthy, and more research on the new factors in our whole environment which are threatening our health.

There are important implications for our health in many of the areas of day-to-day policy decisions in all fields. Decisions about how to tax cigarettes and alcohol will have a direct impact on their consumption and on the serious health damage which is linked with both drugs. Environmental measures to control air, water and other pollution will determine how much we are exposed to low but highly damaging levels of poison. Agricultural policy, much of it determined by the EEC, will dominate the supply of food, its price and nutritional value. The provision of sporting and recreational facilities can help people keep fit and healthy – and this is one of the areas most heavily dominated by the interests and activities of the men, women's sport being very much the poor relation. Transport policy has a vital part to play in relation both to accidents and to air pollution. Decisions about energy sources will determine whether we are exposed to extra radiation from nuclear power stations.

A positive health policy has to cover wide areas of government, local authority and other activity, going well beyond the 'health' facilities which merely patch up the casualties of unhealthy practices in our society, economy and whole environment. Obviously, the many causes of ill-health are not well understood, but there is plenty of evidence to show that certain fairly recent innovations are very harmful, while there are simple policies which can be adopted that will bring known health benefits. We should remember that the dramatic reduction in death rates during the nineteenth century, for example, had little to do with progress in medical treatment and everything to do with improved water supplies, sanitation and housing conditions. It is environmental health measures (largely the responsibility of the local authorities) which guarantee our freedom from major epidemics like those which raged for most of our history. New measures to improve environmental health are urgently needed to meet the present-day threats to health from pollution and other hazards. Let us take a few examples.

Air pollution, or 'smog', in cities during the 1950s and 1960s, is now widely acknowledged as the cause of a number of deaths, and serious respiratory problems for many more, when concentrations of industrial and domestic smoke got to a certain level. Clean air legislation seemed to remove this problem, leaving our cities and towns much cleaner and healthier places. However, in the United States urgent warnings are now being issued for people to stay indoors on days of high concentration of vehicle exhausts causing 'photo-chemical smog' in certain weather conditions. The dangers of adding lead to petrol, which in turn releases high concentrations of poisonous lead into the air, are now well known and a strong campaign is under way to eliminate this unnecessary additive and save children in particular from a substance which probably causes mental retardation as well as other physical damage. As yet, there is almost no recognition of the dangers in Britain of all the other poisonous elements emiting from vehicle exhausts, or of the smoke poured out by heavy goods vehicles running on diesel fuel which is turning the Clean Air legislation into a farce in areas of heavy traffic. The Government scientists, heavily influenced by the roads lobby, are deliberately siting their smoke detectors well away from the main source of smoke, the main roads. Until there is public pressure to investigate the effects of diesel smoke and other exhaust gases, and to impose tight controls, the air we breathe will contain increasing amounts of pollutants, some of them known to be poisonous and perhaps causes of cancer, as well as others whose health effects have still not been properly investigated. Anybody who spends any length of time in heavy traffic becomes aware of the immediate effects – breathlessness, headache, lethargy and so on. What is less obvious is the long-term effect of continual exposure, for example from living on a main road. To this we can add the very serious effects on mental health of loud noise, arising out of road traffic or from planes passing low overhead. It is well established that the areas around airports, for example, provide more than their share of psychiatric patients, especially the women who spend a lot of time in their homes.

Another vital factor in promoting health and the normal development of children is nutrition. There is a large body of research indicating the importance of diet in physical and indeed mental well-being, and the serious implications of nutritional deficiencies for the developing foetus and for small children. Some of the worst deficiency diseases, such as rickets or beri-beri, are rarely seen in this country, but these represent extreme cases of a health problem which can still involve greater susceptibility to illness generally. The only time when there has been a serious nutritional policy in Britain has been during and after wars, when a rationing system has been in operation. It is very interesting to note that during and after the Second World War, at a time of severe food shortages, the overall health of the population seemed if anything to improve. This was almost certainly the result of better distribution between rich and poor, and the policy of eliminating refined and processed bread and other foods, which are very poor sources of essential vitamins and minerals compared with unprocessed food such as vegetables and brown bread. A similar influence could be exerted by a positive pricing policy for food which makes processed junk full of sugar, harmful fats and chemical additives more expensive than the basic foods with a minimum of processing. It is ironical that nutrition is an unfashionable subject, politically speaking: but many women are very interested in food and certainly much better informed about it than many of the government agricultural 'experts' who dictate our food policy. There was a time when one of the biggest elements in government policy was a commitment to cheap food – seen as very much a women's issue. That has now been reduced to rather pointless arguments about the price of butter and how it is affected by the EEC's Common Agricultural Policy. The CAP is in fact a vivid example of a policy which vitally affects women being set without any consultation with us.

Health and safety are often economic issues. Women are forced by job discrimination into a limited range of jobs where we have little bargaining power to insist on healthy working conditions. In retailing, for example, women are often forced to stand for hours on end, with serious damage to their feet and legs. An 'enlightened' employer, such as Marks and Spencer, will provide chiropodists to patch up the painful consequences. Office jobs are often surprisingly hazardous, and the introduction of new equipment such as Visual Display Units, with no limit on the hours of work spent with them, can be a serious threat to many women's eyesight. Many industrial jobs may involve the use of poisonous chemicals which provide short- and long-term health effects, and have particularly damaging consequences for babies born to the people exposed to these chemicals, men as well as women. Health and safety at work are a major preoccupation of the trade unions, but the fact that so many women remain unorganised means that we still have less protection than men.

Various forms of addiction are well known causes of illness and social disturbance, and they can be seen as issues where women's points of view need to be heard. Alcoholism, for example, has been the subject of massive protests by women. The temperance movement, very much a women's movement, has been one of the biggest and most sustained political and social campaigns of the nineteenth and early twentieth centuries, resulting in our present restricted licensing laws for pubs and their opening hours which were pushed through Parliament by the first woman MP, Nancy Astor. Then and now, alcoholism among men has been closely linked to men's violence against women. Now, though, it is women who are becoming addicted to alcohol with very serious consequences to them and their families. The same is true of cigarette smoking where the heavy advertising by tobacco companies, aimed at women and girls, is showing its effects with rapidly rising lung cancer, heart disease and respiratory disease rates among women, which are approaching those of the men. Women seem to find it harder to give up smoking than men once they start, perhaps because of greater stress.

A special addiction problem for women, often combined with drink and cigarettes, is the dependence on tranquillisers and other drugs which are irresponsibly prescribed by GPs for depression. Every year, one woman in eight will take a daily dose of these drugs for a month or more, enough to become addicted. 78 percent of all prescriptions issued are for women, most of them for the drugs heavily advertised by manufacturers as the cure for depression and any other form of mental distress. Yet the cause of the problem is women's overwork, isolation, lack of money and personal mobility and the low value which society puts on our work: all of these problems are essentially political. Many of the health problems facing women arise out of disregard for our needs and choices on the part of politicians, who are claiming, but failing, to represent us.

Health is one of the most crucial issues for us: control of our own fertility, a strong NHS which gives proper priority to our major health problems, preventive health services and information, and action on a broad front to make our lives and our whole environment healthier. It is not merely our own health that concerns us: if *any* member of our family is ill or has some physical or mental disability, we have to shoulder the burden. Women therefore need to become much more involved in decisions on health policy at all levels. Our lives depend on it.

Resources

There are so many pressure groups and campaigns on health issues that it is impossible to try listing them here. A good list of organisations appears in what could be seen as the bible on women's health: *Our Bodies, Ourselves.* The British edition of the work started by the Boston Women's Health Group is edited by Angela Phillips and Jill Rakusen (Penguin, London, 1978).

Two groups, however, stand out as vitally important: the National Abortion Campaign (NAC), 374 Grays Inn Road, London WC1; and the Maternity Alliance, 309 Kentish Town Road, London NW5.

There is an interesting review of seven common medical problems, their causes, treatment and possible alternatives in *It's my life doctor*, published by Brent Community Health Council, 16 High Street, London NW10, price 50p plus postage.

For a healthily disrespectful view of the medical 'experts', see Barbara Ehrenreich and Deirdre English, *For her own good: 150 years of the experts' advice to women* (Pluto Press, London, 1979).

A new look at our mental health, which argues that the way women are supposed to be and act is not good for us, is Jean Baker Miller's *Toward a New Psychology of Women* (Pelican, London, 1976). If you are a doormat, you get trampled on.

5

Education: For Whom?

Some of the biggest battles over women's rights have been fought over education, from the nineteenth-century fight to get women access to universities and professional training to the current campaigns for more pre-school education, an end to discrimination between girls and boys in school, and real equality in higher education. Yet the educational system in this country remains very largely a men's and boys' institution, taking very little account of the need for girls and women to have real choices of our own. Child care and education research and theory, based largely on the need to help boys, have done enormous damage not only to their sisters but also to their mothers. Education is not only a children's issue. It also sets the limits of what is possible for women.

Some of the issues which affect women most seriously are hardly considered in the 'education' debate at all. For example, the age at which a child starts compulsory schooling; the provision of day-care centres, playgroups and other services for the under-fives; transport to and from school; the provision of school milk, lunches and perhaps other meals; school hours; the timing of holidays and half-term breaks – all these fundamentally affect the lives of women with dependent children. The idea that women have to find jobs that 'fit in' with school hours and school terms undercuts our personal freedom and, crucial to many low-income families, our earnings.

We could be demanding that the education system should provide a service to cover the whole normal working day, plus a bit extra for the parent's travelling time, at least until men take equal responsibility for combining their work with responsibility for their children. Extra burdens are being imposed on mothers all the time, such as having to make a packed lunch or provide a cooked lunch for schoolchildren every day: each time the price of school meals goes up, and quality falls, more women have to take on this chore. School meals have in fact been the worst affected element in the education budget cuts of recent years. School holidays, a mother's nightmare, may be necessary for the children and teachers, but holiday recreation programmes should be provided for the children as an essential service to safeguard the jobs of their mothers. The majority of women with school-age children do in fact have a paid job. Even for those who do not, a proper recreation programme for school holidays would mean relief from the tensions which are created from having children at home all the time. Spending time at home could become a matter of choice, not compulsion, and the quality of our relationship with our children would surely benefit. The youth service is failing to provide the facilities most urgently needed, and its preoccupation with organised sports and other activities for adolescent boys is leaving many children and teenagers, especially girls, with nowhere to go out of school.

There is a great deal of what can only be called propaganda about the supposed 'maternal deprivation' that will be caused in children if a mother is not at home in the afternoons when they return home from school, and particularly if she does not spend almost every minute for the first five years of their lives constantly available to them. This theory plays a large part in the argument that women should stay 'at home', in effect housebound, and give up our chance of a paid job. The personal cost to women in this position is enormous, not only in terms of lost earnings but also from the loneliness, frustration, depression and loss of self-confidence which result from unpaid work at home with little recognition and no support – and no regular time off. The 'maternal deprivation' theory, not to put too fine a point on it, is a fraud. The evidence on which it is based, John Bowlby's observations of multiply deprived and disturbed children in post-war refugee camps and orphanages, has been exposed many times over as completely irrelevant to the specific question of how much time a mother should spend with her children. Many child-care specialists would agree that it is the quality of the relationship that counts, for both parents and any other adults involved with the child, and that spending virtually every moment of one's time with a small child is likely to create a strained relationship and difficulties for the child as well as the adult.

For many politicians, 'maternal deprivation' is taken as some kind of Holy Writ, a very convenient excuse for the failure of successive governments and many local education authorities to provide pre-school care as part of the basic education service. It also serves as a great excuse for discrimination by employers and by the further education system to refuse women equal access to jobs and training, if we have children or might have some in the future. Men, according to this line of thinking, have no children – although there is plenty of evidence that a father who 'heads' a family but is hardly ever there, or neglects his children when he is, in fact disturbs them quite as seriously. It is high time the education system and the employers threw out the now discredited idea that mothers should be available to their children 24 hours a day, while fathers have no responsibilities for spending any time with them at all.

A good start: nursery education

Care and education for the under-fives is now increasingly being recognised as a women's issue, essential if we are to have a free choice about our paid work and our commitment of time to being with our children. How ironical, then, that the golden opportunity for expanding educational provision for under-fives which has been created by the falling birth-rate and emptying classrooms in primary schools has been frittered away in a wave of education cuts, redundant teachers and school closures and mergers – often accompanied by bitter battles as parents try to keep their local school open. If only the resources and the classrooms freed by the falling numbers of primary-school children had been switched to new infants' classes for three and four-year olds, we would all be much better off. The failure of the political system to reflect women's need and demand for pre-school education is a reflection of our political weakness. The great achievement in this whole area has in fact been winning the battles to stop the closure of existing nurseries and other facilities. Well organised campaigns are now in existence for proper provision for under-fives, which should provide the basis for an expansion and rationalisation of the service in the next few years.

Day-care facilities for small children are a matter of concern not just for women who happen to have had babies recently. As long as men make no concession to the needs of small children, and in fact usually work exceptionally long hours at the kind of age where they become fathers, child care is very much a women's issue. The earnings gap between mothers and fathers is perpetuated because the enforced absence of women from the labour force while their children are small means not only a loss of wages for those years, but a disadvantage which persists for life in terms of a setback in grade, earnings, prospects and finally pensions. Recent research in the United States has indicated that the effects of withdrawing from a job because of children, together with lower levels of education and training due to a general anticipation of this interruption for younger women, account for up to half of the difference between women's and men's earnings throughout their working lives.

As long as men do not, individually, leave their jobs to look after their small children – a big commitment in terms of time and work – the book *Nurseries Now* suggests that:

> The case for nurseries, at its most basic, is that they provide *one* means of sharing this heavy burden, so reducing the overload on women and its damaging consequences.

It is quite clear that women want nursery or other day-care provision to help with their burden. A 1974 survey by the Office of Population Censuses and Surveys found that a place of some sort was wanted by the mothers of 90 percent of the children aged three to four, and 46 percent of those aged two or under. The findings were the same throughout the country. Even without a paid job, mothers wanted the time free of small children to rest, or do the basic housework that is difficult with small children around. Most of the women surveyed also wanted to return to paid work, not just for the money but for a relief from the monotony of one-to-one dealings with small children and for renewed involvement in society generally, the 'real world': to make this possible a nursery place could be essential. Probably over half of all mothers have at least one job before their children reach the compulsory school age, and this proportion is increasing – it is already much higher in urban areas where it is relatively easier to get jobs.

Women are voting with their feet – back to paid work. If we are asked, we will vote overwhelmingly for day-care places for our small children, in spite of all the guilt-inducing propaganda about our being 'bad' mothers if we ever take a break. For too long it has been the men in government, local authorities and the education establishment who have decreed what *they* think is good for the children *we* are responsible for. It is time that women who are mothers, and who are supposed to have some instinctive gift for sensing and responding to small children and their needs, claimed the benefit of this knowledge: the right to decide.

The advocates of more and better provision for under-fives are not calling for this to be compulsory, although their opponents quite often accuse them of this. In fact, several of the recent books have been pressing for more flexibility and a real choice of service, to allow the mother to decide when the child should start, for how many hours a day, and whether in a formal or informal setting. At the moment the facilities are not only difficult to obtain, but they offer only very limited hours of operation which may be at the wrong time for the women's other responsibilities, and they are very inconsistent from one part of the country to another. Wales is far ahead, Scotland next, and England last. Many rural areas have almost nothing available. Some local authorities are responding to government grant cut-backs by reducing provision for under-fives, while others are building theirs up and paying the penalties. At national level, too, there is a split in responsibility with the DHSS providing pre-school 'care' and the Department of Education and Science pre-school 'education'. There are different training and working conditions for 'nursery nurses' and 'nursery teachers'. If there was this kind of muddle and unfairness in any other sector of education, it would be the subject of furious debate at a political as well as educational level. It is high time, as the campaigners argue, for a thorough review of the facilities which are now available in order to make sure that there is the same range of choice for all those who are responsible for small children.

Part of that review should cover the role of individual child-minders, many of whom are unregistered. Government policy has ensured the mushrooming of private and unregulated child-minding by forcing many women to stay at home and so accept the care of other people's children for lack of any other option for earning money, and by denying the parents who use child-minders any better alternative. There is disagreement about whether child-minders should be taken seriously and provided with training, support, toy libraries and other facilities in order to improve their conditions of work and the care they are providing for their clients. As long as the supply of properly funded and equipped nursery facilities is overwhelmed by the demand, child-minders will remain a fact of life, especially for those mothers who take a job in order to keep the whole family at a decent standard of living and who are forced to rely on neighbours, relatives and other women to look after their small children.

At the other end of the scale, the voluntary playgroup movement is very important to women who live in suburban areas, with higher incomes but virtually no nursery provision. It is estimated to cater for about 600,000 children. This cannot be a complete answer either, since lower-income families cannot afford the time or even the small fees for these playgroups. They could only cope with the areas of greatest need if they were free and had professional support from teachers and social workers – in other words, if they were integrated into the education system of the local authority.

More money and greater political priority must be put into sorting out provision for the under-fives and ensuring greater fairness between different areas and different social classes. The voluntary sector has indeed been crucial in providing some relief from the intense isolation of women with small children, and has developed a style of parents' participation which should be a feature of education for all children, especially at the under-five level. But like so much voluntary activity, it does not have the resources to provide for everyone's needs, especially in the most deprived families. Voluntary groups for under-fives can in fact benefit enormously from injections of money and expertise from the official education system, and the women who have given so much of their time and energy to playgroups could be freed to campaign on a more political level for the needs of their small children as well as a range of other issues which are of concern to them.

The argument for statutory provision of pre-school services for all who need them must be based on the interests of women – because we are forced into such exclusive and unbroken contact with our small children, without help or support, to a degree which is probably unprecedented throughout history. It must therefore mean that the mother's own well-being, or lack of it, will have a powerful impact on the child. One study showed, for example, that when mothers were depressed the accident rate for their small children was four times as high as when they were feeling good. Unhappiness and frustration for a mother is also known to be linked to behaviour problems in children, which makes the task of looking after them even more overwhelming. Many flats are very unsuitable for small children since they are too small to allow any separate play-space and there is nowhere safe for the children to play outside. Trying to keep children in such conditions for long periods is a recipe for boredom and disruptive behaviour on their part, and despair for the adult trying to cope with the endless housework as well as keeping the kids out of mischief. Any change of scene, and more space to play, would be a relief to all concerned in such circumstances. At the very least, a nursery can provide an environment and new companions for play and stimulation which is not available in a cramped home. While nurseries are not necessarily a panacea for all the problems of small children, they can offer a great deal of relief from the tension which builds up for both mothers and children at home.

Pre-school education is much more than a child-minding service, however, it is an essential element in the education system as a whole. A big American programme known as 'Headstart' showed that children from deprived backgrounds who had received some pre-school education had less need for remedial teaching later on, were less likely to drop out of school, and also benefited from their parents' involvement in teaching them right from the start. Nurseries not only help children to develop, and give their mothers a few hours to rest or do other work, they also provide a great deal of informal teaching to parents who are in difficulties about how best to handle their children and how to help them develop in a constructive and healthy manner, which will improve and not damage the atmosphere in the family. There is almost no teaching, formal or informal, for many children about how to look after younger children and babies; our rigid age-segregation in the education system and the break-up of large family networks by extensive rehousing programmes has meant that many young parents – the fathers even more than the mothers – are very unprepared for bringing up children.

Public investment in pre-school facilities is also beginning to be recognised by some local authorities as good value for money, since it can save some of the disruption as well as the expense for social service departments in taking children into care when parents cannot cope. A study by Devon County Council in 1979 found that areas of the county with the fewest nursery-school places had the largest proportion of their children in care. As the level of pre-school provision had increased over the previous four years, 'so demand on other services has reduced'. A continued expansion could produce big savings to the local authorities, both in cost and in terms of human happiness. The whole community benefits if small children who might be in danger of developing anti-social and destructive behaviour, a threat to women in particular, can be given help and relief from family pressures. As in the field of health care, prevention is very much cheaper – and

71

I REALLY WANTED TO BE A MECHANIC
BUT THERE WERE NO APPRENTICESHIPS FOR WOMEN

healthier – than attempts at a cure after the damage has been done.

A fair deal in the schools

What are they teaching our children in school? We may well ask, and the question has hardly been put at all so far: what the schools are teaching our children about us, their mothers, and women in general. It is about time we did take a look, since the text books and many of the teachers are constantly reinforcing messages about women which we cannot possibly accept. From their very earliest years, children are given stories about families in which Dad goes out to work, comes home and reads the paper, and Mum slaves away at home as a personal servant to him and the children, especially the boys (the girls help a little with the work as they learn what *their* life is all about). Story books and lessons are full of men and boys – and the women are almost invisible, certainly not important or interesting, people the children can safely ignore except in doing the cooking and cleaning for them. Later on, when boys and girls are separated, the boys understand that domestic science is demeaning for them; they will only learn 'important' things like technical drawing and science.

Mothers, who have frequent problems with rude and thoughtless sons, could take far more interest in this pattern of laziness and contempt for 'women's work' which is being taught to boys in the schools. They certainly have enough problems getting boys to do their share of the housework and coping with the fierce resentment of girls at their brothers' privileges, without allowing the education system to drive the wedge between them even deeper. The stereotyping of women and girls has been recognised by many to do great damage to girls in school and their prospects over a whole lifetime, but even more serious perhaps is the effect on overworked mothers of the teaching, both explicit and in the 'hidden curriculum', that is being given to the boys. They hope their sons will grow out of their hostility to women but most men never do.

The question of educational opportunity for children is a hotly contested political issue, but the divisions between girls and boys have not been properly recognised as part of the overall debate. Massive battles are being fought over private versus State education, and the inequalities between schools within the State system. Parents rightly take the education of their children very seriously, since this is the key to their whole lives. Yet, until now, the ideas about women being taught to both girls and boys, and the discrimination against girls, have hardly been noticed by many parents, let alone brought out as part of the debate about schools in general.

What there has been, and this has so far gone unrecognised as a political choice, is a strong preference among the parents of girls for single-sex schools, whenever there is a choice between these and the co-educational ones which are now becoming standard.

In certain areas with good girls' schools the parents have voted with their feet – or their daughters' feet – to such effect that the co-educational schools have far too many boys in relation to the girls, something that does nothing for the welfare of the girls attending them.

Although the research on how co-education is affecting girls has only just started to appear, parents have already seen the obvious fact that it can be very damaging to the education of girls, while offering a slight advantage to the boys. This advantage was of course the main motive behind the planners' massive shift to co-education; the excuse in the face of educational losses for the girls is that they derive some 'social' advantage from being with boys. If being treated as inferior, harassed and persistently insulted by the boys, being given much less time and attention by the teachers, and being channelled into dead-end subjects and jobs is a 'social' advantage, then one can only conclude that discrimination is socially acceptable to the researchers and policy-makers who have taken this big decision. It has been observed that co-education based on the advantage to the boys has meant more, not less divisions between them and the girls, more concentration of resources and facilities on the boys, and less choice and opportunity for the girls than they got in single-sex schools. The compulsory dropping of important subjects at an early age, combined with timetabling 'boys'' and 'girls'' subjects at the same time, have the effect of dividing the two into completely different areas of study: science, maths and technology for boys, and shorthand/typing, general arts subjects and housework for girls. When an enterprising girl tries to do an important subject such as technical drawing or carpentry, she is often put at the end of the queue for places in the class, and if she gets in she is subjected far too often to nasty comments from the male teachers about her abilities and even her identity.

Girls manage to do remarkably well in school despite the lack of help and encouragement, but all too often in subjects that will not get them good jobs. The pressure to drop out of mathematics, in particular, is an educational handicap that closes many of the avenues with the best prospects and the easiest promotion. The problem is compounded by assumptions in the career counselling services about 'men's jobs' and 'women's jobs' which effectively channel the girls into low-pay areas such as office work, catering, child-care, shop work and so on, where they will be trapped in boring and inferior jobs that are far below the academic potential that they have shown in school. Unlike the boys, girls in many schools see their future as a complete blank: the educational system offers them no expectations, offers, challenges – or encouragement to meet one should it arise. How do we feel about schools that offer our children no future?

Parents will have to take the lead in questioning the practices of their Local Education Authority (LEA) and particular schools within it. Education is so decentralised that pressure needs to be applied at the local level, just as it is so effectively used in opposing school closures, for example. There are ways of becoming a school governor, as a parents' representative or the nominee of a political party. Schools are also very dependent on the co-operation of parents, especially mothers, in raising money for facilities not provided by the regular budget or helping children with projects organised by the teachers. We should be far more definite about our own priorities, and not allow ourselves to become used as unpaid appendages of the school, which the local authorities have a statutory obligation to finance to an adequate level. We should be campaigning, for instance, about false subject choices imposed on our children, forcing them into ill-considered channels of employment at far too early an age, rather than propping up the budget for an existing, unfair system. Parents could discuss the curriculum with sympathetic teachers, and also with the children themselves, especially the girls. A few schools are making very useful efforts to bring girls' opportunities up to the same level as the boys'. Until now this initiative has rested largely with a few committed teachers, and there is a great need for more involvement from the parents.

In particularly blatant cases of schools discriminating against girls, there is the possibility of going to court. Test cases under the Sex Discrimination Act are needed not only to back up individual complaints and clarify a section of the law which is still largely untested, but also to remind the education authorities in the most forcible way that the Act does contain provisions for equality in education, and that this means *them*. The EOC has been widely criticised for its failure to take strong action on educational issues – although its information service is extremely useful – and more pressure is needed on it to get funding and legal support for court cases. At the same time, the Act itself needs to be amended to make quite clear that, as specified in the Race Relations Act, the idea of 'separate but equal' education is discriminatory, and that separate provision of different subjects for girls and boys is intolerable. The positive action provisions should also be applied to education, to allow planned programmes for redressing the balance of time, attention and opportunity that has been so heavily weighted against girls so far. The EOC should be given the power to issue non-discrimination notices in the public sector of education in the same way as it already can in the private sector.

A second chance?

The British education system is one of the most rigid in the world with its insistence on a fixed sequence of courses and exams, without any break, as well as the premature specialisation in a few subjects with almost no thought or counselling, thus drastically limiting the choices for the whole of one's educational and working life. Opportunities for getting back into the system, after a dropping out which was perhaps the result of a sudden impulse or personal crisis, are very limited. While school-leavers who have passed the right exams have the great advantage of an automatic local authority grant for most further and higher education, someone trying to get back into the system is much less likely to get any financial support, especially when the Government is cutting the local authorities' rate support grants. The victims of this extremely rigid system are, naturally, the women.

However quickly we are able to eliminate discrimination against girls in schools, itself a massive task, the achievement will do nothing for those women who have already been through the system. It will also have no effect on the favouritism towards boys which is shown in the pattern of day-release courses and sandwich courses, as well as apprenticeships, where training is closely tied in with job prospects. There will need to be considerable pressure brought to bear on the whole field of further education to give equal access to all without financial or any other form of discrimination – and without the open bias against women with children which is so often a feature of admissions practices of institutions.

Where genuinely open and equal access is available, we find that women form a large proportion of those involved. Local authority and university extension evening classes have always had a preponderance of women. This sector, which is the key to re-entry into education for many women, is also among the hardest hit by the education cuts. Another area of opportunity for women is the Open University, where the largest single group of applicants is made up of 'housewives', the second biggest group are clerical workers and office staff, a group which has suffered particularly from the lack of career opportunities appropriate to their ability due to their lack of encouragement at school. Altogether, in 1981 women formed about 45 percent of Open University applicants, but on the introduction of higher fees resulting from cuts in government funding, many dropped out because they could not afford to pay.

A series of changes will be needed in the whole of further and higher education to give women a better deal and enable us to make up for the losses suffered as a result of inadequate provision in school. There are already many opportunities of particular value to women (the EOC is a good source of information) and these should be much more widely publicised – in launderettes, health centres, nurseries, primary schools and supermarkets, as well as the traditional secondary schools and libraries. Particularly important are the basic training or 'foundation' training courses designed to remedy lost confidence, low aspirations and a difficulty in studying, as well as basic mathematics and technical skills necessary for getting jobs so far denied to us. Programmes for these kind of courses include 'NOW' (New Opportunities for Women) and 'WOW' (Wider Opportunities for Women).

We need a greatly expanded provision of courses at all levels with much more flexible entry requirements to help women join, especially as mature students. The fees for such courses should not be set at a level which excludes women. Courses should be at the right times for those with children (given the present ridiculous school hours, courses should be between 9.30 am and 3 pm in the afternoon). There should be a creche for small children. Provision will also have to be made for time off during pregnancy and after the birth, as a normal occurrence, not an educational crime. In fact the whole idea of taking time off when necessary, and building up course credits as and when convenient, needs to be introduced into our system. It already exists in many other countries, together with a standard system for transferring from one institution or course to another when the student has to move. Special efforts should be made to encourage students into fields previously seen as closed, or alien to women, if necessary by special courses planned in order to counteract the discrimination which until now has kept us out. There is specific provision for this in section 47 of the Sex Discrimination Act, and much more use needs to be made of the possibilities here. Those in charge of the further education sector should also be working on industry and commerce in order to get women as well as men on to meaningful day-release or block-release courses.

Because of the importance of post-school education in helping women to catch up from previous disadvantage, Dale Spender (in *Invisible Women*) has suggested that the country actually needs a new Education Act, to replace the 1944 Act and its amendments which set up our whole present system of school education. A new Act should formalise the right of all individuals to education and training at any age, as the only way forward for the 'lost generations' of women who have not so far benefited from the Sex Discrimination Act or Equal Pay Act because of their inadequate

77

schooling and therefore poor job opportunities and prospects. This could be the most effective of all proposals for positive action for women.

The teachers

Teaching has always been a women's profession, from the governesses of private education to the elementary school teachers at the start of our present education system. Today women constitute virtually all nursery teachers and nursery nurses, the great majority of primary and middle-school teachers, and many of the teachers in secondary and further education. A much smaller proportion have jobs in higher education. Women training in teacher-training colleges have always been of a higher overall standard than the men, because of the lack of access and encouragement to get into universities and polytechnics. Yet throughout the education system it is men who decide what will be taught, how, and to whom – based on their own rather limited knowledge and experience which contains almost no understanding of the needs and potential of girls. There is a rapid decline under way in the number of women in senior positions in our schools and colleges, with the retirement of older teachers who are not being replaced by promotions among the younger ones. This is a particular feature of the rush into co-education, where headships and positions of Head of Department are being overwhelmingly allocated to men in preference to women, except in the 'girls' subjects' which are not seen as important. The men are increasingly imposing the difficult but less prestigious jobs on women, including 'pastoral care' of children with problems, dealing with parents, and having to take responsibility for all the girls even if they are not teaching them or responsible for the boys in the same class. This is yet another example of the exaggerated sex stereotyping which is being imposed in the co-educational schools. Girls in the school are only too aware that women get all the problems and none of the credit, and also that a woman is not permitted to have authority over boys however well qualified she is. This is yet another lesson in their own inferiority and educational irrelevance in schools where the real task is seen as teaching the boys. The importance of senior women teachers as 'role models' for the girls has been highlighted by many investigators, and if the men teachers treat their female colleagues as anything less than professional equals this has a powerful impact. The boys, too, are only too alert for the unstated messages conveyed here, and the denial of authority over them to any teachers who are women can only exacerbate problems of discipline in a school as well as a mother's authority over her sons. It can do nothing but harm to the attitudes of the boys towards women and girls in general; indeed the issue of boys' harassment of girls, and of many female teachers, has become a serious one in many mixed schools.

If parents are to intervene successfully to improve their daughters' chances in these schools, they will have to take up the issue of appointments to senior positions and allocation of responsibilities, supporting the claims of the women teachers. It is likely to be a bitter battle in some areas, since many mixed schools are now boys' schools in which girls, and women teachers, are treated as marginal. Even worse is the position of women who are teaching in all-boys' schools. The takeover by the men has gone so far that a number of girls' schools are starting to appoint men as Head Teacher and in other powerful positions.

The teachers' unions, of course, have a crucial role to play in getting a fair deal for their women members. It is not merely a question of appointments, promotions and the allocation of specific responsibilities. Many of the men are earning more money than women at the same level because different subjects are now being valued at different rates. It comes as no surprise to learn that it is the 'men's' subjects which are higher paid. The option of retraining women who already have good teaching abilities and could easily switch subjects has been given very little priority, although the results would compare very favourably with the present inequitable system. Another blatant injustice in the pay of women in education is the pathetic wage and inadequate training given to nursery nurses, who could be said to have the most important task of all in dealing with sometimes difficult children and getting them into the habit of learning which will be needed through their educational career.

It is a well-worn cliché in the politics of education that parents need to work with teachers if the children are to get any real benefit from the school, and to make any sense of the connections between school and home. Mothers, who have primary responsibility for the children and who are invariably blamed if anything goes badly wrong with them, will have to make common cause with the women teaching their children if effective action is to be achieved to correct the imbalance in educational provision and the distortion of attitudes in boys as well as girls. And for those women whom the system has already failed, we should all be campaigning together for a post-school education system available to us as of right, to give us a second chance.

Resources

The EOC has a number of interesting publications on education, including *Equal Opportunities in Post-School Education* whose recommendations could revolutionise further and higher education if they were properly implemented. The EOC can also provide advice and sometimes legal support for presenting complaints about discrimination in education, and it keeps a register of opportunities for women to get a 'second chance'. The address of the EOC is given on p. 17.

A useful guide is Harriet Harman's *Sex Discrimination in School: How to fight it*, published by the NCCL (for address see p. 17), price 75p. Harriet is now a Labour MP.

Much of the evidence about discrimination against girls in schools is presented in Dale Spender's *Invisible Women: The schooling scandal* (Writers' and Readers' Co-operative, London, 1982).

Eileen M. Byrne's *Women and Education* (Tavistock Publications, London, 1978) provides a round-up of many of the issues discussed in this chapter. There is also a very useful collection of essays in *Learning to Lose: sexism and education*, edited by Dale Spender and Elizabeth Sarah (The Women's Press, London, 1980).

A campaigning work on pre-school provision is *Nurseries Now: A fair deal for parents and children*, by Martin Hughes, Berry Mayall, Peter Moss, Jane Perry, Pat Petrie and Gill Pinkerton (Penguin, London, 1980). If that inspires you, the National Childcare Campaign is based at 17 Victoria Park Square, London E2.

6

Traffic: Have *You* got a Company Car?

I was in the middle of reading up some books on transport policy when I went out shopping, on my bike. I had just passed one of the familiar yellow accident markers, calling for witnesses to a road accident. As I waited at some traffic lights I saw a motor-cycle cross – then suddenly an elderly woman was in his path. She saw him, but could not move fast enough. He knocked her down. She lay full-length in the road, quite still, as I leapt off my bike and ran across, then back to a pub on the other corner to ask some workmen to ring for an ambulance. One of them already had; the others looked round curiously at me, surprised that I should be upset. It was only an old woman knocked down in the road.

When I got back, she was lying across the road wth a pool of blood under her head. The motor-cyclist was distraught, unable to help. Meanwhile the little group of people was blocking the road, and cars started hooting. The man in the front one edged past, a few inches from her head, the thin exhaust pointing down at her.

The motor-cyclist kept asking, 'Will she be all right?' I tried to reassure him: the light had been green for him, it was his right of way. She should never have crossed because the traffic was always coming, from different directions, and there was no safe time for her to cross over to the local shop.

Then the police came, and I offered a statement as a witness. They were surprised that I had stayed; judging from all those yellow signs, most people do not bother about road accidents they have seen. And if it is just an old woman being knocked down, what are they supposed to do about it?

The policeman asked me if I knew this road, Camden Road. I certainly do. It is an old road with plenty of 'improvements' to speed up the traffic and increase capacity for the commuters at

81

peak hours. It often has these little yellow signs announcing an accident. It also has old people trying to cross it, painfully slowly. They have always lived around there, and leave home just to get to the shop on the other side, or the little park where they sit listening to the traffic noise when it is warmer. It is quite an ordinary main road for London – or Birmingham, Liverpool, Glasgow or any other big city.

The street scene

If you want to see inequality in our society today, look out in the street. Better still, walk down to a major junction. See the cars and lorries speeding past: the objective of all traffic planning is to keep them moving, as fast and freely as possible, and to eliminate 'conflict' with people on foot. Most of the cars are driven by men, especially at peak times, and many of them carry no passengers. A number of them are a special breed of pace-maker, powerful cars accelerating hard driven by young men for whom this is a 'company' car, a perk of their job. Any damage to the vehicle is charged to the company, not to them. Is it my imagination that some of them seem to accelerate as they drive straight at the women in the road?

In town centres the people endlessly waiting to cross the street, or hurrying across between breaks in the traffic – they are mainly women. Some are carrying heavy bags, some have small children and are coping with a push-chair or shopping cart. There are older children on their own and teenagers, together with pensioners – women and men – and a few people who are blind or have other disabilities. The pavements are too narrow for all the people on them, and any pram or wheelchair causes an obstruction. People are hemmed in by metal barriers set into the pavement, making it even narrower. They are forced to climb up and down steps to get over the traffic, or down dark underpasses. In some places the pavements are blocked by parked cars, and women are forced to wheel their babies into the path of the traffic. Then there are new obstacles set into the pavements all the time, traffic-control posts and boxes, a nightmare for blind people. In order to provide a free run for the men in their cars, the space for women to walk on – or to stop and talk, or sit in – is being constantly reduced.

From time to time somebody on foot tries to reclaim the old freedom of movement, and some of their wasted time, by crossing the road where it is most convenient. They risk being killed or badly injured. In any collision between an 'unprotected' person and a car or lorry, it is almost always the person on foot who is hurt. Whenever I see drivers putting their foot down as they rush through town centres full of shoppers and other pedestrians, I remember the old woman I saw knocked down as she tried to cross the road in the old way. The penalty for this, too often, is death. Our streets now compare with those of imperial Moscow or Petersburg where the carriages of the aristocracy would drive at reckless speed, horses trampling the people to death beneath their flying hooves.

Motor vehicles are by far the biggest threat to life and health in modern society, infinitely more than the violent crime on which politicians focus. Contrary to general belief, it is mainly people without cars who get injured and killed in the streets. In 1980 there were 6,010 deaths from road accidents, and almost two-thirds of them, 62 percent, were *not* in cars at the time: most were on foot, some rode bicycles or motor-cycles. Children are particularly vulnerable, with 500 of them knocked down by vehicles every week. In addition to all the deaths, thousands of people are paralysed or permanently disabled as a result of their injuries. In crude financial terms, 1980's accidents alone are estimated to have cost us £2 billion, which takes no account of the pain and suffering of the victims and their relatives. We are too used to seeing danger on the road as a problem for car drivers. In reality, it is their cars that have become the killers. It is very rare to have accidents involving passengers on the railways – but when that happens it is headline news. The routine toll of 17 deaths and almost 1,000 injuries *every day* on our roads, a total of 325,000 casualties in 1981, has never become a big issue for the press or politicians. It is high time that we made it so.

The power of the planners

Transport planners have been given free rein to design our towns and cities, and large areas of the country, around cars and lorries. Inner cities have been blighted by plans for new roads, traffic management schemes, roundabouts, urban clearways, ring roads, overpasses and the rest. Roads have been widened, houses knocked down and slices cut into or through our parks. By-passes and motorways have been the subject of bitter controversy, which until recently the technocrats always won because they wrote the rules and made the traffic 'forecasts'. The result has been noise, pollution, obstruction of walkers and cyclists, an enormous number of deaths and injuries, and congestion which *reduces* mobility even for car owners. New schemes designed to speed up traffic in one place have been found merely to lead to increased bottlenecks somewhere else. Britain is now probably the most heavily congested country in the world.

It is people who suffer in a system designed by technocrats for the welfare of machines. In particular it is the women who lose out. The National Travel Survey of 1972 showed that three-quarters of all adult women aged 17 to 65 have no driving licence. If you add the older women and girls, the vast majority of us are unable to drive. At best we may sometimes be passengers in a car which someone else controls, and we cannot call on this service as and when we need to travel. Some women with licences do not have regular access to a car at all. Married women with a share in a car usually drive it only when their husbands do not want it, and in many cases the machine is parked at the man's place of work or clogs up the neighbouring streets during working hours. In central London, half the available parking space is occupied by cars left stationary for eight hours at a time. If it is a company car, it may not be insured for family members to drive it. Apart from the tiny minority of married women who are in two-car households, there is a very small number of women who own a car in their own right.

In terms of getting where we want to go, then, most women have to do without a car either some or all of the time. In trying to achieve some kind of mobility we are the victims of the planners' obsession with cars, men's cars, and badly affected by the deteriorating range of facilities within our reach whether we are walking, taking public transport or trying to ride a bike in the middle of it all. It is difficult and dangerous for us, but even more important, it is hell on wheels for our children. Deaths on the roads are by far the largest category of child mortality, despite all our precautions. This means that when children are small, they have to be taken to school or anywhere else they want to go, even to visit friends a few streets away. It also means that we cannot risk allowing them out of the house or garden to play in the street, so they wear us out getting under our feet all day. This factor alone must be to blame for pushing many depressed and overworked women with children into mental breakdown, or the addictive drugs which a visit to the doctor will so often bring.

The power of the transport planners is such that although access to basic facilities is of vital concern to everyone and affects our lives profoundly, we do not have to be consulted about their plans. The House of Commons went for ten years without transport policy being mentioned, except in passing, until January 1977. During those ten years, actions of national, regional and local government seemed dedicated to setting in ugly concrete a whole range of traffic changes, costing us billions of pounds, which were all based on a series of misunderstandings by the planners of how people actually get around.

In fact, by far the most important means of transport is our own two feet. On average, each person makes one journey every day entirely on foot. This means over 48 million journeys every day in Britain, one third of all journeys and almost as many as the journeys made by car. To this we must add walking which is part of a trip using public transport or cars. Separated out into stages, we find that walking has overall a 49 percent share of all travel, compared with only 35 percent for cars and 12 percent for public transport. The great majority of the journeys on foot are made by women, with the most important reason being shopping. It is startling to find that shopping on foot, overwhelmingly done by women, is one of the two most important single reasons for personal travel, and is only just behind the major one, travel to and from work. Public expenditure on pedestrians is minimal, amounting to about half a penny per journey, and we can compare this with public expenditure on each car journey of about 25 pence, mainly in terms of roads and traffic systems. Provision for men's journeys, it would seem, is fifty times more important to the public exchequer than provision for women; and this take no account of the costs inflicted on the community by the use of cars, or the enormous tax subsidy paid out on company cars.

Successive governments, under intense pressure from the self-appointed roads lobby, have produced a totally false picture of our real transport needs, and managed to exclude in the process most of women's needs. A 1978 Government White Paper, the aptly named *Policy for Roads*, falsely claimed that four-fifths of all journeys were being made by car; in fact this was more than double the real percentage. It even suggested that half the journeys in households without cars were being made by car, although in fact the proportion is about one in eight. An investigation by the Policy Studies Institute in 1979 found that official miscalculations about how people travel had been blindly incorporated not only into all national transport planning but also into town and country planning at national level, the work of many other Whitehall ministries, and the preparation of local traffic schemes by County Councils and local authorities.

The mistakes arose out of the decision to exclude from the calculation all journeys on foot (but not by other means) if they were less than a mile long. This is the majority of all walking trips, and they account for some of the most important journeys of all: shopping; visits to post offices to collect pensions, child benefits and other vital payments; journeys to school, which women often have to do in order to ensure the safety of smaller children; and a lot of the journeys to work. Ignoring the importance of walking, planning departments in every field are making women's lives more difficult by reducing the number of facilities within reasonable reach on foot. Schools are being closed down, doctors' surgeries and chemists' shops are fewer (but larger), local employment opportunities in urban centres are drying up, post offices are being closed, and there has been an enormous number of closures among food shops, which women rely on for providing their families' daily needs.

If food shopping is being planned by the companies on the basis of a massive drive-in, then not only do corner shops close down as they lose some of the customers who keep them going, but prices at the local places also rise in relation to the big supermarkets. On top of that we are forced to take the bus to get to a decent shop, which costs us more money, especially with some fares going the way they are. It costs us more of our precious time, not to mention the aggravation of terrible bus services and tubes, which are a special nightmare with small children. For some women, especially in the country or the outer suburbs, the family budget is knocked completely out of balance because they have to have a car to get anywhere. Mainly because of this, household spending on transport rose from 8.3 percent of the total budget in 1958 to 13.4 percent in 1970. Whichever way you look at it, increased planning for cars makes women worse off. Jobs, too, get harder to find as they are moved out on to a ring road or the main road to somewhere else, instead of within walking distance or on a bus route.

As if that were not enough, we are paying taxes which help subsidise the company cars, the ones that are the worst driven on the roads today because whatever happens, the company (and the government) pays. The subsidy has been estimated at £1,500 million a year. That's just a start. Then there are the constant million-pound rescues of British Leyland. The amount we have been spending on motorways and new traffic schemes of all kinds, let alone maintenance of the existing network of roads and bridges, is incredible: in the mid-1970s new construction was about £700 million, maintenance £340 million and administration £88.4 million. In the United States and elsewhere, lorry and car drivers pay for new super-highways through tolls. In Britain they are a free gift, from us. Aren't we generous.

The roads have grabbed land from densely packed urban housing, eliminated thousands of acres of prime farm land, ruined many of our parks and parts of the countryside with the noise and smell, and carved up cities and country areas alike. No longer is it 'the wrong side of the tracks'; our own areas are now divided by the main roads. Children, especially, are almost imprisoned inside a tiny area by busy roads running all around. There are many other costs, in money and in human terms. There is the staggering cost to the health services, especially emergency facilities and long-term rehabilitation for people paralysed or maimed in accidents. (We won't count the grief of people bereaved in this way, since the planners give no cash value to that). We also have the menace of lead poisoning, leading to mental retardation and perhaps delinquency among city children. As we have seen, mental breakdowns are known to be greater in areas subjected to constant loud noise, whether from airports or, more usually, main roads. The officially permitted noise level from a heavy lorry getting moving at a traffic light is the equivalent of standing just behind a Jumbo jet when it takes off (if you live near a lorry route you won't need telling). And in 1983 they actually *increased* lorry sizes and weights permitted on our roads, and may do so yet again.

The lorry lobby is one of the most powerful of all, and seems to have completely captured the Ministry of Transport. Increasing road freight has been accompanied by a steep decline in rail transport for which the facilities already exist, and the virtual collapse of coastal shipping which is much more efficient for many journeys. The growth of road transport has also contributed vastly to the sprawl around our towns and cities. The amount of goods being carted around the country has increased very little, but distances have increased enormously as companies move out along the new roads so that we are all now subjected to constant unnecessary freight movements right past our own front doors. The problem cannot be solved overnight, because the process of motorised sprawl has already gone a long way down the road. We need to bring it back: oppose any increase in weights, insist on strict testing of all lorries on the roads for safety, noise and weight, make sure the drivers are working reasonable hours, and then tax the owners so that they pay for the full cost of injuries and deaths they cause, the nuisance to people from fumes and noise, the damage to roads and bridges, and the inconvenience to residential communities of having to provide precious road space for the monsters. This will be an incentive to the companies to decentralise, move closer to their markets, provide jobs nearer home, and reduce their demands on our environment.

One estimate, by an official of the Department of Air Resources in New York, is that in the United States the real cost of road transport by cars and lorries amounted to the staggering figure of between £75,000,000,000 and £150,000,000,000 a year, gobbling up between one-sixteenth and one-eighth of the total wealth created in the whole country. In case those noughts do not mean much, there is an estimate from our own Transport and Road Research Laboratory that the annual investment in new roads in Britain is matched by the annual cost of road accidents alone, in terms of lost output, hospital care, police and law court time and destroyed property. It is perhaps just as well for them that they have not tried to estimate the total cost of damage by cars and lorries here, because the total would be so staggering that we might just decide to jump off that particular bandwagon and ditch the roads altogether.

Meanwhile, there is no money in the Government's kitty to mend the pavements for the millions of pedestrians, to provide a safe network of bike lanes, to keep a good service of buses running, with reasonable fares, or to invest in freight movements by rail, sea or canal.

Reclaim our streets

One of the reasons why it is so difficult to tackle the problems of transport and traffic is that different sections of road are controlled by different authorities: local Councils, Metropolitan and County Councils and, for the biggest and nastiest, the Department of Transport. We desperately need a more localised control over our streets so that people can go straight to those responsible without constantly being referred to some higher authority. Adding to the complexity of the issue are the special formulae, traffic counts and jargon used by the engineers and planners, who are often very unsympathetic to people's demands for better access, road crossings and improved road safety. At the same time, in many areas they have been able to demolish whole areas of a city or town, or produce planning blight in the name of a future road widening or other 'improvement'.

It is important to remember, though, that the public authorities at all levels have already been successfully challenged on many occasions. A large proportion of the ambitious road schemes of recent years have been altered or cancelled because of opposition at public inquiries. All over the country there have been successful local campaigns to oppose road-widening, impose local lorry bans, install pedestrian crossings and close off commuter 'rat-runs' that bring danger and congestion to residential streets. Women have played a leading role in these campaigns. It is quite exhausting to be involved in traffic planning on a local Council, since this issue arouses tremendous passions in people, perhaps more than anything else a local authority does. People who for years have felt oppressed and overwhelmed by the traffic and the seeming impossibility of getting anything done about it are getting together to demand improvements to cut down accidents, pollution and noise. There is a great deal that can be done at a local and regional Council level – but finally the problem is one of national policy.

Many of the problems of enforcing safe driving and parking laws are the monopoly of the police, who in some areas have virtually given up despite public concern about it. Not only do the police look the other way when there is dangerous driving and obstructive parking, but sometimes they are themselves seen driving at reckless speeds which endanger other road users. The police are under no obligation to enforce parking control that a local authority might see as essential for safe access to schools and hospitals, emergency access routes, or to facilitate deliveries in an important industrial area. Councils in urban areas are paying out large sums for traffic wardens who are ineptly managed by the police, reflecting the low priority which the police give to traffic control. Unlike other police officers, the wardens are very poorly paid and work with little supervision or encouragement, and have no contact with other organisations or the local authorities who are most concerned to regulate parking in the interests of all road users. Unlike the police, wardens can be, and are, abused by those they observe breaking the law, and violent attacks or threats of attack on wardens are frequent. The routine issue of two-way radios and immediate back-up in difficult situations is not extended by the police force to their wardens, many of whom are of course women. Traffic and parking control would be done much more efficiently and responsibly by the local authorities which should have the power to employ wardens, plan an integrated programme of traffic law enforcement linked in with their existing powers to define parking control zones with meters and yellow lines, and also fix their own penalties for parking offences, and be free to collect the fines with full reimbursement of the costs. Traffic control in congested urban areas is a complex matter, but vital to the local economy as well as to everybody's well-being generally: sophisticated management is essential, at the local level.

The courts also have a vital part to play in cutting the huge costs, human and financial, of reckless driving and parking. More court time, and more efficient procedures are needed to reflect a greater priority to restoring real 'law and order' on our streets. A recent decision of the French supreme court, the Cour de Cassation, could provide the model for a new approach.

As *Walk* magazine reported in March 1983, the judgment reversed 50 years of decisions in favour of car drivers who had injured or killed people with their vehicles. It made drivers of motor vehicles automatically liable for damages to any other road users not in a motor vehicle if they damage them or their property. The liability is automatic and unlimited, unless the driver can prove that the 'behaviour of the victim' was 'unforeseeable' and 'irresistible'. In other words, people in charge of the dangerous machinery which today's vehicles are will be held responsible for any damage they do with it, in all but the most exceptional circumstances. It removes the machines and their users from their previously privileged position as the only objects with which you could hit someone without having to accept liability for the injuries or damage caused. Other countries, too, are beginning to take a much stronger line on the legal liability for damage done by cars: in the United States, fatal accidents are increasingly likely to be treated as homicides, and the penalties for drunken driving are being made far more severe under pressure from public opinion, especially the women in MADD (Mothers Against Drunk Drivers) whose children have been killed or injured, or who are threatened by dangerous driving.

In Britain there has so far been little change, and women will have to become far more assertive on this issue if we are to achieve greater safety for ourselves and for all the most vulnerable people in our society. The preoccupation with drivers' safety, especially in the campaign for seat-belt legislation, fails to provide any benefits for all the other road users. Old people may react or move too slowly to escape a speeding car, whose driver perhaps feels more secure in his seat-belt. Blind people and others with disabilities are at such a disadvantage that they may be afraid to use the streets at all. Children are very much at risk since they do not develop the judgment to assess the distance and speed of an approaching car until quite a late stage. The streets are extremely dangerous for all these groups. Too often many people's response to busy, noisy roads is not to go out, not to walk or ride a bike, and to cut down on the physical exercise, the social life and the general sense of freedom that we could otherwise enjoy.

Air pollution and noise are also issues that require strong action. We have heard a great deal about the effects of lead, a petrol additive which is recognised widely as a serious threat to our health. However, there are many more elements in the exhausts of both petrol and diesel-powered vehicles which have hardly been investigated at all. Just consider, for example, that one of the easiest ways to kill yourself is to inhale the exhaust from your car. Possibly even worse are the clouds of smoke emitted by diesel engines, producing levels of many pollutants which include suspected cancer-causing chemicals. The only standards now being applied to diesel smoke are related to how visible it is, only the thickest and blackest clouds are illegal, and even here there is very little enforcement. The same is true of noise, especially the low-frequency vibrations of heavy goods vehicles which are literally shaking people's houses to pieces along the main roads.

What we most need is an integrated transport policy that shifts the financial incentives away from cheap road freight and the inefficient use of private cars towards other means of transport. It will mean much greater support for public transport: a fast and reliable service that everyone will be happy to use. It will be much nicer and cheaper to get on a bus or train than to fight the rush-hour commuter traffic; it will be a pleasant walk through streets which are not clogged with vehicles that do not need to be there. Residential and shopping areas would have their own delivery routes for small vans away from pedestrians, and there would be special routes for clean, quiet buses, bikes, disabled people's vehicles and emergency access for ambulances and fire engines. There would be more space in the streets for people to walk, children to play, grass and trees to grow, and benches for people to stop and stare. We could start to reclaim the idea of a street as a place for people to meet. Lonely people could be a bit less isolated. Children could get around safely. The mental health of the whole community, as well as the physical health and safety of each individual, could benefit enormously from such a transformation.

Utopia? But it is clear that people are desperate for an escape from increasing fumes, noise, danger, and the problems of trying to get around. Time and again, it is women who are in the forefront of demands at the local level for a relief from traffic. We have the worst of the deal in both ways: we are hemmed in by the problems of traffic, and we are immobilised by our own lack of a car and the decline of local services and public transport. If we are to reclaim our streets and with them the quality of our lives, we must make transport a women's issue at national as well as at local level.

Resources

The Pedestrians' Association, 1 Wandsworth Road, London SW8, has campaigned for many years, on very limited resources, for the people on foot in streets designed for cars and lorries.

Friends of the Earth are at 9 Poland Street, London W1. They are the most comprehensive environmental organisation with a strong position on transport policy including pollution problems, freight movement, campaigning for cyclists and so on. There are many other groups, national and local, dealing with related issues: try the library for a local list.

There is an excellent survey of the importance of travel on foot in *Walking* is *Transport* by Mayer Hillman and Anne Whalley (Policy Studies Institute, 1 Castle Lane, London SW1, 1979) available at £3.50. If your interest is bicycles, try Mike Hudson's *The Bicycle Planning Book* (Open Books, London, 1978).

Two other background books are John Grant's *The Politics of Urban Transport Planning* (Earth Resources Research, 40 James St, London W1, 1977), price £2.50, and Terence Bendixson's *Instead of Cars.* This was published by the Scientific Book Club, London, in 1975 and is unfortunately out of print, but public libraries could get it if it is not in stock. A wealth of ideas about the alternatives, from a writer who now chairs the Pedestrians' Association.

7

Housing: A Woman's Place

If Britain really is 'two nations', the divide is greatest in housing: owner-occupiers on top, and Council tenants underneath. It is hardly ever recognised that women are much more dependent than men on Council housing, and whether we live in owner-occupied or privately rented accommodation we have less security there than the men. Housing is very much a women's issue.

During marriage, women obviously have the same housing as their husbands. But much of this is still in the husband's name alone, whether it is rented or owned, or provided as part of his job. Although the law made great strides in the 1970s to give women rights over the family home, many are still not aware of the possibility of joint tenancies or ownership, and lose out when it comes to separation and divorce, or the death of the husband or partner. Single women still suffer discrimination in housing, and separated or divorced women are often forced out of the privileged world of the owner-occupiers into local authority or privately rented flats. Local Councils are having to provide accommodation for an increasing proportion of the women with children who form single-parent families. Between 1967 and 1975 the numbers of women in this position, receiving supplementary benefit and living in a Council flat, nearly trebled. There are also many women among the homeless, both single and those with children. And lesbian women, with or without children, remain among those facing most discrimination in housing.

Some of the 'disadvantaged groups' known to have special housing problems also contain many women. Of the twelve main categories identified in official reports, seven include more women than men. Only three – ethnic minorities, students and mobile workers – have more men. Two of the groups have equal numbers: younger single people, and large families. The seven with a majority of women include the largest categories: the elderly, lower-income households, single parents, the physically disabled (with many women crippled by arthritis and rheumatism), people facing violence at home, those officially classified as homeless, and the mentally ill or handicapped. The numbers of women in these categories alone run into many millions.

The immediate problems of housing people in need belong to local authorities, and it is here that action is needed to ensure a fair allocation of resources. As a local Councillor, I have found that the majority of people coming for help are trying to get their housing problems sorted out. Many of the women involved are desperate. Whenever I get someone coming to my 'surgery' who says they are at the end of their tether and cannot find anyone who will understand, they are astonished when I guess they have a housing problem. It is not just a question of a shortage of housing, but the lack of a 'human face' to housing management, which operates in a very bureaucratic and masculine way. A few examples will illustrate the problems of people with nowhere to call their own.

A married couple in a nicely re-done house wanted to move half a mile to an empty place exactly the same, in the street where the woman's physically handicapped sister, her brother suffering from bouts of mental illness, and her elderly mother who needed help getting in and out of bed, were living. The housing officials had refused the move as 'low priority'.

Another woman with an elderly mother and a seriously ill aunt on the same estate was desperate to move out of her two-bedroom flat into a nearby three-bedroom. She and her husband had to share their room with a four-year-old girl in order to give the young teenage son some peace and quiet for homework. She whispered to me that the marriage was breaking up because they had 'no family life you know what I mean?' I was not able to get her a transfer; she was labelled as 'too fussy' because she insisted on staying near the old people she was looking after.

An old and dilapidated estate was due for rehabilitation. I got an urgent message that old and housebound people who had lived there for decades had got eviction notices, and were terrified of having to go to court. The housing office protested that this was a formality: of course these silly tenants would be rehoused, what were they getting worried about?

A woman from Sierra Leone with a sick husband and three children had been evicted from her flat because the DHSS had stopped paying the rent while she was in Africa for a family crisis.

For months she had been in short-life housing, overcrowded, freezing cold and with a leaking roof, constantly being moved around. The officials took months to reply to an urgent appeal for the right to permanent housing so that her children could settle down properly somewhere, and the family get their affairs sorted out with the social security office instead of the constant problem of claiming afresh from different offices.

A woman in her fifties was desperate to get her daughter, young husband and their new baby out of her own flat. The overcrowding and quarrelling was threatening to break up both families at once. At the same time, a young woman in a 'shared singles' flat was struggling to get a place of her own before her baby was born, but was held back by the rent arrears piled up by her former boyfriend, now disappeared. A young woman with two children living in a refuge for battered women in a different Borough (to get away from her violent husband) wanted to come back to the area she knows, but at a reasonable distance from him. She was not on the doorstep of the Housing Department, so she had been forgotten.

This is just a small sample of the housing cases arising constantly for women dependent on Council housing. Others were desperate about getting repairs done, vandalism on the estate, nowhere for the children to play, complaints about noise, worries about the rent. Housing management is in a dreadful state in almost every local authority, especially the big cities. Is it coincidence that this field, exploding in size and importance after the Second World War, was taken over by men from the women who had managed it before and during the war? There had been an emphasis on integrated management, inspired by Octavia Hill with her insistence that the person you pay your rent to should also be responsible for the repairs and upkeep of the property. Another of her ideas was the emphasis on preserving an existing community, even where the housing conditions needed improving. This concept was swept aside by the new male generation of housing planners, who destroyed much of our city centres in the name of 'slum' clearance and built acres of faceless tower blocks which are now being acknowledged as a disaster, not only for their effect on family and community life but even in their construction and financial viability. Whole populations have been despatched, without consultation, to new estates and new towns away from family and friends – and often far from any possible employment or basic facilities like transport or decent shops.

The original emphasis on public housing as a social service has also been swept aside by the rent-collector mentality. Many of the housing officials seen on the estates are ex-policemen whose job is purely to chase up the rent, without any responsibility for the services being provided or the particular housing needs of the family. As Council rents have been forced up by the Conservative Government's withdrawal of subsidy, tenants find themselves paying extortionate rent and rates with very poor housing conditions in return. Many Council rents are now much more than mortgage payments would be, since there is such a heavy and increasing subsidy through tax relief for owner-occupiers. The rates, too, are generally higher for Council tenants since their flats are regularly revalued while many houses in the private sector are being assessed at the rateable values of ten or 20 years ago despite very large rises in their value.

The Conservative Party sees the answer to the tenants' problems in the 'right to buy' their flat or house. The idea certainly has popular appeal although the actual number of sales is very small in comparison with the original claims about who could benefit. Local authorities are understandably resistant to the idea that they should sell some of their best and newest properties at cut rates, with no compensation from the Government for the loss made. The prospects of a move to better housing are dwindling for the great majority of tenants as the Council stock of houses dwindles, while the old flats are all that is left. A few privileged people who could afford to buy on the private market get a great bargain from their right to buy at a discount, at the expense of everybody else in the public housing sector, and especially the low-income families who could never get a mortgage, where women are the great majority. Subsidies for owner-occupiers with mortgages were worth £1,614 millions in 1979/80, and rising rapidly, while subsidies for Council tenants are dwindling, and Government grants to urban authorities have been savagely cut. By 1983, subsidies for owner-occupiers were four times those to Council tenants. If the tax relief for mortgages were redistributed to all tax-payers there could be a substantial cut in income tax, to perhaps only 20p in the pound as basic rate; then everyone would be able to afford decent housing, whether rented or purchased, and house prices might fall without the subsidy for loans. Better still, there could be a big increase in personal tax-free allowances, which could enormously benefit low-income people and reduce the enormous housing gap between rich and poor.

Such a move would give a much wider choice to more people

between paying rent or a mortgage, and the phenomenal rent arrears now threatening to bankrupt local authorities would certainly be reduced. Bringing housing subsidies under rational control, and providing special housing help to the people in special housing need, is essential if all women are to have decent housing.

Anybody who can get a mortgage is now being forced to tie themselves to buying a house, whether this is the best choice or not. The present system is inflexible, but also very insecure. There is no acceptable 'safety net' in the form of private rented accommodation, which is almost non-existent for anyone with a low or even average income. Housing associations are booked up solid, and many have even closed their waiting lists. Decent Council housing is very hard to get if you are trying to move from one place to another. Far too many people are forced to mortgage their entire working lives to a house or flat, when they would be better off, especially when they are starting out, in a modest rented place. If your home goes with your marriage or even your husband's job, as so many do, then the pressures to stay become overwhelming even in situations of violence or extreme unhappiness. Housing policy in this country is not meeting our needs. Instead, it is forcing us to invest far too much, our whole future as well as our money, in only one of our basic needs at the expense of others, and especially at the expense of our freedom of movement.

The fear of homelessness goes with the fear of destitution, for many women in particular. If you have no fixed address, it is hard to get your social security. It is virtually impossible to get a job. The many young women who are homeless in the big cities are especially vulnerable to being recruited into prostitution, from which it is then hard to escape. Older women who are homeless often suffer from periodic illness, which makes it all the more difficult to find a way out. Many are hidden away in psychiatric institutions and hospitals. Homeless women with children, some of them evicted for their husbands' rent arrears, stay for long periods in overcrowded and soul-destroying local authority hostels. Some Councils split up the family, excluding husbands and even the older boys from the family hostels, and the punitive attitudes of the old workhouse are found in many. The Government has issued circulars recommending minimum standards, but has not been prepared to enforce these, so that many local authorities are failing to observe even these mininal safeguards. It is no wonder that many of the women find their children being seriously disturbed by a stay in the hostels, their possessions lost and their family broken up permanently as shown in the 1960s television film, *Cathy Come Home*. Cathy was never able to come home – it was broken up by the housing system, as so many others still are.

The fear of being driven into such a situation, with its inevitable humiliation and threat of utter despair, certainly forces many battered women to cling to the homes they have, however unhealthy this is for them and their children. Some have been forced by the Council to stay with violent men who finally beat them to death, or caused serious injury. This is surely an indictment of our whole housing policy, and especially of our failure to provide enough refuges and emergency accommodation as well as good, secure housing for longer-term moves for women and their families.

Designing a home

It is extraordinary that housing and flats are planned by men with so little consultation with the women who will spend so much time in them. This applies to private house building, but even more so to Council estates. Normal household activities like drying the washing seem to be completely forgotten, forcing many women to buy tumble-dryers which use a lot of energy and make potentially damp flats even worse. Space for children to play, within sight of their mothers, seems to be ignored by Council architects, who may give the entire space to car-parking. Proper security is overlooked by the planners, who install cheap, flimsy front doors and windows. Over and over again, there are complaints about the inadequate kitchens in Council flats, the rooms where women do so much of their work, but do not have enough space to do it properly. There is not enough storage, especially for prams. The flats are often very expensive to heat properly, which means staying cold, skimping on food and clothing to pay the bills, or facing the devastating effects of being cut off. Outside, the whole environment of an estate is often dangerous, with dark corners making it too easy for women to be attacked. Estates are built with little regard to transport, shopping and employment. It is often suggested that the architects responsible should be forced to live and work, with children, on one of their prize estates.

People prefer to be at ground level, and in many cases suffer severely from having to climb the steps that architects think so much of. Elderly and disabled people may become housebound for no other reason than the failure to provide level access or a

ramp to the front door. The daily struggle of carrying a shopping cart, pram or small children up and down steep steps is one that is imposed quite unnecessarily on many women. Many housing estates are inaccessible in other ways: finding the way to a particular address can be a nightmare on a big estate. Important services like refuse collection and the delivery of milk and post can be hampered by ignorant design. Even the street, for so long the focus of social life and design interest for architects and residents alike, has been destroyed. A lot of the recent housing turns its back on the street, with blank walls – an invitation to graffiti – and an accumulation of garages and back-door rubbish which shows the contempt of many planners for the community which they are supposed to be serving. If only the people themselves, and especially the women, could be involved in judging new housing, perhaps after a year of living in it, then we would have a completely different list of design awards. Housing standards, too, would stress the convenience to the occupier of a flat or house, and the vitality of the social life of the estate or street it belongs to. Some of the old patterns are still the best-loved, especially the row of front doors facing the street, or a square with all front doors facing inwards, while safeguarding the privacy and security of the household. A mixture of people, adults, children, old people, provides a living community, much better than the ghettoes of single-parent 'problem' families, old people or young singles which are all too common in modern 'planned' living.

The stereotypes of our planners actually leave no room for real people and our peculiarities. Women with growing children would benefit from being able to move the walls to meet changing family needs. Many single people, especially young women who cannot afford to buy their own flat, want to get a room of their own in a shared flat or house, yet there is no official recognition of this trend in new housing design. Older people in their own houses need help with repairs and maintenance: not just the grants, but practical help in getting the right contractors and supervising the work. Physically handicapped people, especially the elderly, need more practical help in converting their homes to their changing needs, a service which is available only patchily. None of these requirements is considered in the standards for housing, based on the 1961 Parker Morris report, which assumes that all households are two-parent families with dependent children, with the mother staying at home full-time to look after them. Design guides used for planning family housing give a picture of family life with the mother always waiting on the other members of the family. If this is indeed the case, and Mother never leaves the house except with the children, the standards are totally inadequate. They enforce isolation of the family, a recipe for mental disaster, with no facilities for shared child care or meeting other women in the same grim situation. Those on low incomes are marooned in faceless blocks, while those who seem better off in terms of family income may be even worse off in their suburban isolation or on new private estates with virtually no community facilities or playgrounds. The area where the family lives, as well as the kind of housing, is almost totally related to the needs and aspirations of the husband and his job. If housing policy were more flexible, the women would have a better chance of deciding how, and where, we want to live.

Housing action

Building societies must take a large share of the blame for our housing problems. The societies take huge sums of money from small investors, including countless pensioners, and women saving what they can 'for a rainy day', and invest the whole lot in housing the people who need help the least. This is a betrayal of the ideals of their founders, who were poor people joining together to get their own houses. Societies are not accountable to their investors, and pursue their own planning policies by, for example, 'redlining' whole areas of our cities where they will refuse to lend money. This has led to the loss of hundreds of thousands of good houses available at reasonable prices. The societies are also very restrictive in whom they will lend money to, demanding evidence of a steady income of the kind that many people, especially women, just do not get. They reject older people, the self-employed, those on low incomes and the unemployed. Until not long ago they discriminated openly against women, and a recent investigation by the EOC showed that many societies and individual branches were still doing so. Discrimination against women, or couples where the woman was the main income-earner, was shown to be especially common in the Cheltenham & Gloucester, the Woolwich Equitable, and many of the smaller societies.

Past and present discrimination by the building societies means that very few women own a house or flat in our own right, while those in owner-occupied houses are very dependent on their relationship with their husbands, who are in many cases the sole owners of the property. Fortunately, the law is catching up with reality and married women have recently acquired important rights to stop their husbands selling the house or using it to secure their own loans; and to live in the house with the children if the marriage breaks up. There are also other groups of women whose right to their home has been much neglected: those living with elderly dependants, who often find themselves on the streets after the traumas of a terminal illness and death; and women living together in a lesbian relationship. Many women in various different situations are still not aware of their rights to the family home, or ways of keeping it going if the husband is no longer paying the mortgage charges. A big information campaign is needed to make sure that women can secure their rights to joint ownership of the family house. The rights of women who are living with a man in a joint household also need to be properly secured, by new legislation. An Englishman's home is no longer his castle only – he should be sharing it fully with an Englishwoman.

But ownership can never be the whole answer for people who are increasingly mobile. The rented sector is in desperate need of investment, mainly by the public sector which has for too long been starved of money now being diverted instead to subsidise interest rates for owner-occupiers. Funds have been further reduced by very high interest rates which local authorities have had to pay over a number of years on the capital borrowed, with absolutely no relief from central Government on that interest. There may well be a case for scrapping housing subsidies altogether, since everyone needs housing and it is a nonsense to speak of everybody paying more tax to make handouts – to themselves. Any subsidy which is given to housing should go to the public sector to house people in special need for reasons of disability, old age or low incomes – mainly women, and children.

At the bottom of the heap are those who are homeless and need short-term emergency provision as a way back into secure accommodation, or who are trapped in homes which have become a prison and who urgently need a way of escape. Housing is the biggest problem for women facing violence from their husbands – often directed also at the children. Most of the women in the available refuges had tried to leave home before, three times on average, and had been forced back to violent homes by having nowhere else to go, or by remaining exposed to assaults because of insecure accommodation where they could be intimidated by husbands into returning home.

There is a desperate need for more refuges for battered women and their children. At the last count, about 200 small refuges, mainly run by volunteers, had sheltered over 11,000 women and nearly 21,000 children. Yet a Select Committee of the House of Commons on Violence in Marriage reported in 1975 that six times that number of refuges were needed. In some areas, the provision is less than a tenth of the established minimum need. Most refuges are severely overcrowded, in a desperate state of disrepair, and vulnerable to closure at any time for lack of money or by order of the local authority. Successive governments have failed to provide the money necessary for this most urgent of needs for temporary accommodation, to rescue the victims of the most common form of violence and abuse in society. It is extremely shortsighted, since the worst problems of health breakdown, disturbed children and anti-social behaviour generally are to be found among homeless and battered people. Spending money now to relieve their housing needs must surely pay dividends in keeping families together, and in the long term preventing the disturbance to small children in particular which could make them a liability to society for a whole lifetime.

A new approach

There is an urgent need for housing investment to be directed more rationally, with special help to those at the bottom end and with the overall aim of eliminating the social 'apartheid' which divides the whole population between grotty Council estates and prim suburban isolation. Whether people rent their homes or take out a loan to buy them, they should feel at home there, with basic services provided as a matter of course. Council tenants in particular deserve a better service, not just in terms of repairs and maintenance but also in the freedom to move, and with direct participation in management through a tenants' association for the estate they live in. Experiments with proper tenants' participation, with control over a budget and over the use of common areas of the estate, are still in their infancy but look very promising as a way forward. 'Sink estates' can be revealed as places of real community life, often showing great concern for the elderly and disabled tenants and organising events for the children as well as physical improvements in the estate which will benefit everyone. Tenants' relationships with the Council employees on the estates are of course a delicate issue for negotiation with the relevant unions, but many employees find their work much more satisfying if they are accountable directly to the tenants they serve, instead of to some faceless bureaucracy operating a system of bonuses and schedules of work that have little to do with the real jobs needing to be done. What is required, overall, is housing management in which everybody has a say – management with a human face.

Council housing, however much it is improved and added to, cannot by itself meet the needs of all the people wanting to rent. Many people, especially single women, remain anxious for a room of their own; many are paying out far more than they can afford on a privately rented but very dilapidated room. It is surely in the rental sector that the building societies should be making their investment, alongside the housing associations, in providing basic housing for rent at a reasonable price. A very modest suggestion would be that at least half their funds should be invested in building and renovating new rental units in the areas of greatest demand, providing a range of accommodation to suit all tastes and circumstances, including single people wanting to share facilities but also have space to call their own. There is no reason why we should not ask for legislation to force the building societies, if they prove unwilling, to share out the savings of their own small investors more fairly in this way.

Effective housing action requires a long-term commitment to new house building and renovation, as well as an understanding of people's real needs. Both major parties have shown themselves very insensitive to this: Labour Governments and local Councils have been responsible for some disastrous 'slum clearances' of perfectly good, modest houses, and put up in their place new housing which is now seen as a social and financial calamity. The Conservatives have savagely cut housing investment in the public sector, and tried to force the sale of existing Council housing to private buyers to reduce their stocks still further, especially of the newer houses. At the same time they have raised the limit on tax relief for private mortgages from £25,000 to £30,000 – hardly a measure to help those in need. They have also imposed sudden freezes on improvement grants and on housing association funds, which have played havoc with investment in private and public rental stock as well as the rehabilitation and repair of old houses.

Both major parties have dithered helplessly over reforming housing subsidies, terrified perhaps of upsetting the man in 'his' subsidised castle. They have set arbitrary 'cash limits' which prevent Councils from rehabilitation and new building in the inner cities, where it is most expensive. Each freeze on grants, loans or investment means the loss of thousands of homes, often in poorer areas with the greatest housing need. Houses start to collapse very quickly after basic maintenance stops and cold and damp are allowed to penetrate the fabric. There has to be a long-term programme, with a guaranteed right to the available funds set a few years in advance, to allow time for planning, consultation and construction. We also need a technical assistance programme for those unfamiliar with the work necessary, especially the elderly. For those owner-occupiers or landlords on good incomes, such a service – backed by penalties for those who neglect housing which is occupied by tenants – should in fairness be in the form of guaranteed loans at market rates, rather than the free gift of a grant to increase the value of their private property with no benefit to the community as a whole. There should be much stronger powers, and in fact a statutory obligation, for Councils to take over houses which have been left empty and decaying for more than a reasonable length of time in areas of housing shortage.

Can we break through the destructive cycle of stop-go policies in housing? Can we rescue our existing housing stock and provide a steady supply of new homes, flexible enough to meet the needs of different kinds of people at different periods of our lives? Can we transfer housing subsidies from the richest people to the poorest, especially women with children? Can we get a housing management system with a human face? Can people feel more secure in their homes as well as have the freedom to move?

Perhaps we could move towards this ideal if more women were involved in housing investment, design and management – as professionals but also as people who spend much of our time there. We spend much more time at home than men do, we usually care more about our homes, and we do most of the work there. If women do not insist on a decent housing programme, who will?

Resources

A number of pressure groups for women have a strong interest in housing, including the National Council for One-Parent Families (255 Kentish Town Road, London NW5), the Women's Aid Federations (WAF England is at 374 Grays Inn Road, London WC1) and the National Council for the Carers and their Elderly Dependants (29 Chilworth Mews, London W2).

There are also of course the campaigning organisations on

housing, the best known being Shelter at 157 Waterloo Road, London SE1.

Marion Brion and Anthea Tinker have produced an excellent review of this issue in *Women in Housing: Access and influence*, (Housing Centre Trust, 62 Chandos Place, London WC2, 1980), price £4.90. It includes a look at the women who pioneered public housing provision and management, but who have been virtually taken over by the new breed of male managers who have made such a mess of our homes.

A useful review of women's rights to a house or flat they live in is in chapter 8 of *Women's Rights: A practical guide*, by Anna Coote and Tess Gill (Penguin, London, Third edition, 1981).

Leaving Violent Men: A study of refuges and housing for battered women is a very comprehensive study of the housing problems of this group. It was published by WAF England (see above) in 1981, at £2.

8
Happy Families

So much of our law and national policy is based on the institution of marriage – as seen by the men – that it is fundamental to the treatment women get in such fundamental areas as tax, employment, social security, housing and even personal property. All of these are separate issues in their own right, and are dealt with as such in this book, but policy on marriage and the family is so important that a brief discussion seems to be necessary as a separate issue.

In the lead-up to the 1979 election, 'family policy' became a big issue, presumably on the basis that the male politicians saw this as a way of getting the women's vote. Some quite exaggerated claims were put forward, beginning with the Conservatives' Patrick Jenkin who told us in 1977 that the family 'possesses strength and resilience, not least in adversity. Loyalty to the family ranks highest of all . . .' Not to be outdone, James Callaghan claimed for the Labour Government that 'The family is the most important unit of our community. That is why for the first time in our country, our Government is putting together what amounts to a national family policy.' He proposed a 'Ministry for Marriage', while Patrick Jenkin proposed a 'Family Council' where those concerned could 'bring their influence to bear directly on all ministers whose policies affect family life'. Almost no real discussion actually took place about the different kinds of family, their internal and external problems, and how policies could be improved to help the majority of their members who are women and children. In fact a sudden silence on the family issue descended after the election of the Conservatives to power in May 1979, perhaps because many of their economic and social policies have been very damaging to families, especially those most at risk because of poverty, unemployment, family tensions and break-up, and the individual problems of their members. The issue suddenly re-emerged in 1983 with the leaking to the *Guardian* of highly confidential proposals by the powerful Family Policy Group.

It is important to remember that women are held responsible for keeping families together, and the politicians seem to agree that husbands and fathers count for very little in the family. Some of the discussion about 'the family' is really a discussion about women, and our 'place' as seen by men. Peregrine Worsthorne, an extremely conservative commentator, has advocated that 'the family' should take care of 'the poor', 'the uneducated' and 'the humble', apparently to replace the entire range of State provision. He concludes, in an article in the *Sunday Telegraph* of 6 July 1980:

> . . . it is the rights of the family , not those of the State or the individual, which most need to be strengthened today, since they are what the working man, in the final analysis, relies on most . . .

Women's rights, then, are to take second place to the interests of the working man. We have been warned.

Generally speaking, the periodic rediscovery of 'the family' by the politicians seems to be a way of avoiding any proper consideration of women's interests, as distinct from those of men which have so dominated the whole political process. In the family which the men seem to have in mind, women exist only as supporters for them, not as people in our own right with our own interests inside and outside family life, as the men have. It is revealing that the Study Commission on the Family, set up in 1978 under Campbell Adamson, has representatives of youth groups, the Church, social services, trade unions and others – but not one single women's organisation. This is more than a little strange, since the long established women's organisations such as the Women's Institutes and Mothers' Union represent those women who are particularly committed to their families, most of them not doing paid work outside the home in order to devote all their time to family activities. These women are apparently the last to be consulted about family policy. Still less is there any real consultation with the women who are wholly responsible for almost all the one-parent families, which are in particular need of help and support. Strange?

The explanation for this has been advanced, especially by Jean Coussins and Anna Coote, in terms of the attempt by conservative men in particular to use 'the family', which bears little resemblance to any real family, as the excuse for two kinds of political action.

These are increasing women's economic dependence on men; and abandoning the post-war commitment to public services, the 'Welfare State', which was meant to redistribute money and resources from the better-off to those in need. They also see in much of the discussion about 'the family' an authoritarian attitude, a drive towards an enforced conformity which they see as particularly oppressive in an area of personal freedom such as family life. So, for example, the State is supposed to prevent homosexuals from living together, force unhappy couples to stay together, prohibit cohabitation, and generally police the way that people choose to live with each other. Above all, they are trying in the name of 'the family' to get women out of the paid labour force. As Patrick Jenkin has recognised, 'family life' is changing as a result of women having paid jobs; he has suggested that we give up our claims to a fair deal, or be forced to do so:

There is now an elaborate machinery to ensure equal opportunity, equal pay and equal rights; but I think we ought to stop and ask – where does this leave the family?

Jenkin and his colleagues are also very keen on the idea, despite all the evidence to the contrary, that children will be 'deprived' if they are ever looked after by anyone other than their mother. Any social problem is being blamed on women who have their own commitments outside 'the family'. One wonders, in fact, whether these ideologues would understand why fathers are starting to take more care of their own children, and make a bigger commitment to their families – and whether they would see this as destructive of the 'family life' which they are advocating for us.

Some of the ideas produced by the élite Family Policy Group created by Mrs Thatcher are certainly rather strange. Senior Cabinet Ministers and her personal advisers, meeting regularly to formulate the Conservative manifesto proposals, have discussed how to 'encourage' mothers to stay at home and parents to set up their own schools; questioned the 'professionalisation' of teachers, social workers and doctors who 'tend to undermine individual responsibility' and suggested providing social services through charities rather than as a right; making parents responsible for the anti-social behaviour of their children; abolishing Wages Councils; and providing intermittent work for unemployed family men. Some of the proposals are extremely vague and confused, and some are trivial ('Train children to manage their pocket money,' urges the Chancellor of the Exchequer). However, it is clear that something very important has been going on, since this Family Policy Group has had more influence than the Cabinet in some important decisions.

There certainly is a need for policies which help families, particularly those in trouble and those responsible for dependent children, elderly relatives, or sick and disabled members of the family. The first thing to understand is that there is no such thing as '*the* family', but many different kinds of family with an increasing number of people living alone or in couples, perhaps in touch with their families but not living with them. In 1978, a married couple with one or more dependent children – the 'typical' family of the politicians – actually accounted for less than a third of all households. A family with a single male 'breadwinner' and economically dependent wife looking after children was even less typical. Real-life families include those with a single parent, families with adopted or fostered children, 'reconstituted' families following divorce and remarriage, extended families with aunts, uncles and grandparents, childless couples, those with grown-up children, separated families with fathers being away from home for their work, widows and widowers, single people living with their parents who may be elderly or disabled, brothers and sisters living together, groups of friends sharing a house or flat, and couples – including lesbian couples and gay couples – who are not married, sometimes with children. Over time, families change fundamentally, splitting up and reforming as their members grow up and move out. How can the married man, dependent wife and small children ever again be used as a model for the variety of real families, and the political action needed to strengthen them? We need to recognise all forms of family group. In particular, all women need to defend the right of lesbian women to determine their lives, to choose where and how to live, and to bring up children without interference.

The answer, surely, is to leave families the freedom to do as they like, and to offer services and support that will help them look after their dependent members where they want to do this. In the end, nobody can be forced to look after others, even if they are related; the amazing thing is the strength of many family ties, and the effort and love which are so often given – especially by women – to family members who need it. National policy so far has given very little real support to these women, and any family policy worth the name would involve vastly increased child-care provi-

110

sion, proper home nursing and home-help support, respite care facilities (to give carers the time off and holidays that can make all the difference), and above all the financial support necessary to help compensate for the loss of earnings involved in long-term care of relatives, and the cost of bringing up children. Such important social security benefits as child benefit and invalid care allowance can make all the difference to the welfare of real-life families, as opposed to the cardboard cut-outs of Patrick Jenkin and James Callaghan. Above all, policies to support families in need must be formulated in close consultation with the women's organisations representing those most closely involved in family life, and who know its strengths and weaknesses far better than any politician.

Family problems: women's problems

Leo Tolstoy claimed that all happy families are alike, while unhappy ones are miserable in different ways. We do not have to agree about the fortunate ones to recognise that there are many problems associated with family tensions, separation and divorce. Much of the attention focuses on the problems of children, who can become the target of a custody battle. But perhaps even more serious are the problems of women who have fulfilled all the traditional expectations in giving up their own jobs and interests in order to devote themselves full-time to their homes and families, contributing greatly to their husbands' careers and bringing up their children almost single-handed – only to find themselves divorced after many years of this personal and financial investment in their husbands' interests. The Americans, who have had even more experience of this than we have, call the victims of such divorces 'redundant homemakers', and compare the break-up of the marriage and family to the dismissal of loyal employees who have worked so long for a particular company that they cannot be retrained or re-employed anywhere else.

Much of the debate about maintenance payments, or alimony, misses this important element – it is far too often assumed that any woman can go out and get a job at any time, regardless of how long she has been out of the job market, and that if she does not manage this she must be some kind of a lazy 'drone'. Yet in most cases she has been working hard for many years without pay. A 'redundant' wife loses her job, and at the same time her whole way of life and her security; she is very unlikely to see any of the pension which her husband's good pay will bring in. Any changes in the maintenance procedures at divorce need to take into account the realistic earning prospects of women who have not had a paid job for many years for the convenience of husband and family, as well as the better-known need for her to receive financial support for the children. One approach would be to see maintenance payments to a wife as compensation for the loss of marketable skills and experience, and perhaps the loss of educational and training opportunities resulting from many years' commitment of time and energy to the family. It is not the fact of marriage that would count, but the alternative opportunities lost by taking responsibility for a family. At the moment, the politicians as well as the lawyers

are failing to acknowledge the real cost of this commitment, even while they are urging women to leave paid jobs in order to increase it. Recent proposals by the Law Commission would drastically reduce women's rights to compensation or maintenance from a former husband who had benefited from her unpaid work.

We have moved a long way recently towards the principle of sharing equally any possessions acquired during marriage, or an informal relationship in the case of couples who live together. Women are now much more likely to keep the family home if they also have custody of the children, and judges are biased in favour of the mother in many contested cases although they are still violently prejudiced against lesbian mothers. Maintenance payments are much more of a problem, especially in enforcing the judgment and getting the settlement revised to account for inflation and the changing circumstances of both parties. Far too many women find themselves caught between erratic or non-existent maintenance from former husbands, and the problems of claiming proper social security to fill the gaps. There are several different systems, at the moment, for collecting maintenance either through the magistrates' court or the divorce court. The best system is for maintenance orders to be signed over to the DHSS, which means that the Social Security office becomes responsible for collecting them while the family has an automatic right to weekly payments even if the payments are not made. It would be a simple enough change to make this the standard practice, not the exception.

Men make a great fuss about paying maintenance, and even claim – rather strangely – that women are now 'equal' and therefore should not have any right to maintenance at all. The failure to make regular payments has a particularly bad effect on the children who are usually involved in such cases, and this seems to be another example of the urgent need to make men more conscious of their equal responsibility with women for children they have together. In an ideal world, perhaps the whole of society would take responsibility for young children, making sure that every one had tender loving care and enough money to provide whatever they needed. But this book is dealing with present realities, not future fantasies, and children's welfare is still heavily dependent on their parents. The answer to the husbands who claim to be 'discriminated' against in custody and maintenance payments is that only if they have made the same sacrifices of time, money and employment prospects for the sake of small children and the family home that their wives have made can they claim equal treatment in divorce and separation settlements. It goes without saying that if the husband has put in the kind of effort usually given by women, and his wife has done much less, then he should receive recognition of this in any settlement.

Separation and divorce are at present in the hands of the courts and the 'adversary' system of lawyers representing each of the former partners, who set up a contest over family assets and often the care of the children. Both women and men would benefit enormously from a network of conciliation services which could take much of the bitterness out of the whole process by producing an agreement worked out by all concerned, rather than a decision by a judge in favour of one side or the other in a pitched battle. Women, since we have a greater financial and emotional stake in marriage and the family, have a particular interest in taking the heat out of divorce wherever possible – and we also have to deal more closely with the disturbances produced in our children when they have been the subject of a custody battle. Conciliation procedures can, for example, result in an agreement to share custody, something that the adversary system hardly ever produces. Although almost everyone involved recognises the need for this alternative to the courts, successive governments have proved too mean to provide the necessary funds. This is a false economy, because the real cost of the present system in terms of legal aid, court time and the social work necessary with disturbed or even abandoned children is obviously very high.

Making it legal

For a relationship that is supposed to be private, a refuge from State intervention, marriage is an amazingly rigid institution. The amount of Government regulation of marriage is quite staggering, while the degree of real support for the relationship itself is pitiful. The men who make the rules have concentrated too much on the question of legal paternity, making children 'legitimate' or otherwise, and elaborate rules of inheritance. Women have many other concerns, with a greater involvement in the day-to-day care of children, their emotional welfare and their real – as opposed to legal – relationships with everyone else involved. If the Government is to try and legislate for marriage it should be in the interests of all those involved, and with special emphasis on the welfare of dependants. It is absurd that the men of the Law Commission,

114

formulating new proposals on marriage, should *still* insist on maintaining a distinction between people born 'legitimate' and those born 'illegitimate', like something out of a Shakespeare tragedy with sons battling for the crown of their father. If men are to be important in the lives of children nowadays they must become emotionally involved, and responsible in a complete sense rather than just a financial one.

The aggressive insistence of so many government bodies on distinguishing between the 'legitimate' and the 'illegitimate' is even fiercer in relation to women than it is to children. Many officials still insist on knowing if a woman is married or unmarried, by distinguishing between 'Mrs' and 'Miss'. They become quite hostile, or bewildered, when confronted with a woman's refusal to use either title. They have no difficulty in pronouncing 'Mr' or 'Mrs' but pretend to be incapable of pronouncing 'Ms' as 'Miz'. Many government and local authority departments still resist women's preference about their titles, ask for information about marriage 'status' when this is quite irrelevant to the issue, and impose special restrictions on the rights of women whom they discover to be married such as demanding the husband's consent to her agreements on matters personal to her, including credit or even medical treatment. However, the men are on weak ground. They demand of women a distinction which does not apply to themselves. They are up against a determined minority of women who are quite prepared to create confusion in their careful systems, by refusing to state whether or not they are married and demanding the same rights for all women without distinction. In fact this state of confusion is probably the best result of the controversy, since the present system obviously does not solve the many problems that arise every day over marital 'status'. Confronted with a British Rail clerk who objected to the title 'Ms' on my credit card, I told him with a straight face that having been married ten times, I was getting confused about my official status. He retreated in dismay.

Similar problems arise over women who quite reasonably insist on their legal right to keep their own names, married or not. It is a matter of prejudice, not law, that many official institutions will try to force women to use their husbands' names instead of their own. Plenty of women are quite happy to do this; others are not. A name is the symbol of a separate identity, and adopting a husband's name may not be welcome – in the same way that American black people may object to using a name that was bestowed on their forebears in slavery to match the name of the master.

There are so many official distinctions made between women on the basis of our marital 'status' that it would be impossible to list them all. Tax and social security systems, in particular, provide unequal and unfair distinctions between husbands and wives, and between women who are married and unmarried. But at the same time some of the families under the greatest pressure – ethnic minority families who are especially dependent on family support in the face of hostility from many outsiders – are given no recognition at all for their close personal relationships. A British woman often has no legal right to live in this country with a husband who has some other country's passport. If she has a child abroad they may be separated on return home, since that child has no claim to a British passport. Only a government of men could think up such refinements of discrimination: British men have an automatic right to live with their wives, and they can confer British nationality on their children who are born abroad. Such injustices are extreme examples of what can happen when men make up the rules about marriage.

Although marriage is obviously less stable than it used to be, this contract, which almost everybody signs, but nobody reads, is still of vital importance in defining our rights and obligations in society generally, although it makes much less difference to the men. About 95 percent of women get married at some time or other, some more than once. For many of us, it implies enormous commitments to other people – not just the husband, but our children, and often his elderly relatives. Even brief interruptions of paid work which arise from these commitments can reduce our job prospects and financial security for the whole of our lives. If the marriage ends with divorce it is usually the woman who is left holding the baby, in a much worse position than if she had never married. If she is widowed she receives only the meanest support from official bodies, and enormous problems in a society which has no recognised place for older women by themselves.

It is no wonder that marriage and the family are first and foremost women's issues, even if men are involved as husbands in equal numbers. Their official status is almost unchanged by it, and they are not expected to make sacrifices for it, in fact they would expect to have their comfort and convenience increased by the sacrifices of a wife. The law and custom of the central government, local authorities and every institution in public life, as well as the private domain, are dominated by the men's monopoly of rule-making for their most intimate relationship with women. The traditional women's organisations have been trying for many years to have a serious input into the debate on marriage and family law, with some success but overall much less influence than they should be achieving on this issue. More recently, the new wave of women's organisations and campaigns have added their voice to the demand for women to have an equal say. Any politician who wants our support will have to acknowledge our point of view on marriage as being vitally important, just as our commitment to family life is what keeps it functioning. Just think what would happen if we went on strike.

Resources

For a review of the political and economic implications of family policy, and proposals for a more constructive approach, see *The Family in the Firing Line: A discussion document on family policy*, by Jean Coussins and Anna Coote (NCCL and CPAG, 1981), available from the NCCL (for address see p. 17).

There is a comprehensive list of organisations interested in families and children in Diana Davenport's *One-Parent Families: A practical guide to coping* (Pan, London, 1979).

Useful advice on the legal implications of marriage, cohabitation and divorce is available in chapters 5 and 6 of *Women's Rights: A practical guide* by Anna Coote and Tess Gill (Penguin, London, Third edition, 1981).

A campaigning organisation and advice centre for single parents is the National Council for One-Parent Families (for address see p. 105).

The NCCL Rights for Women Unit is a source of much information on the legal implications of marriage, including a very handy booklet by Jean Coussins called *What's in a Name? How women can keep or change their names* (1981), price 80p.

9
The Sex Industry

Prostitution

Prostitution is a man's world. It is regulated by laws made by men, enforced by 'Vice Squads' of men, judged by magistrates who are mainly men, and organised by the men who own and manage the hotels, bars and sex establishments used for prostitution. Last but not least, the whole trade is supported by large numbers of men, including these same law-makers, police and managers, who pay for the prostitutes' services. Since it has been estimated that one woman in prostitution will deal with an average of fifteen to twenty men a week, it is obvious that the business involves very large numbers of men engaged in prostitution as the paying customers.

Why, then, is prostitution a women's issue? A careful distinction is made by most men between women in prostitution, the lowest of the low, and 'respectable' women. Many of us are embarrassed or afraid to discuss the whole question. But at the same time, there is an increasing recognition that many of us are involved in a form of unpaid prostitution, obliged to put up with sexual manhandling for the sake of our jobs or our marriages – in fact our income, and our whole way of life. Many women seeing a woman standing on a street corner for customers will recognise that 'there, but for the grace of God, go I'. All women are affected by the laws governing the professionals, whether or not we are directly involved. If we are in a red-light district we are likely to be harassed, propositioned, perhaps threatened. We have creeps pestering us, especially from kerb-crawling cars, in the sure knowledge that laws against soliciting are never applied to the men who do most of it (unless they proposition other men). We have to pass sex shops, massage parlours and other places which make us very uneasy. In the inner city, we might find prostitutes and their clients parking outside our windows, upsetting the children, sometimes threatening those who complain. As the clamp-down on prostitutes working in Soho or Kings Cross heats up, the business moves out into new residential areas: our street or area can be taken over by the men's sex business, becoming virtually a no-go area for most women at night.

Many men will suggest, with a snigger, that the answer to all these problems is legalised brothels, like the Eros Centres in West Germany which are set up and organised under the scrutiny of the State. However, far from solving the problems of blighting whole areas for women, they reinforce this by creating zones no women will want to be seen in. For the prostitutes themselves, wherever they are able to express themselves, they show complete revulsion at the operation of these institutions, or of the semi-legal brothels which operate under the 'protection' of powerful men in the key positions. The women involved are dehumanised, exploited ruthlessly, stripped of their last vestiges of dignity and choice (no client can be refused, nor can any of their demands), and virtually imprisoned in the building. Many of the women will risk the known dangers of street soliciting, where they can be exposed to savage attacks and murder, to avoid the horrors of the sex factories.

Women have to discuss prostitution because until we start to define a policy and practice for the authorities the situation can never improve, and at times of economic recession and un-employment will become much worse – with young girls being forced on to the streets if they leave their homes or cannot find a job. The basic cause of prostitution – sex for money – is that men have the money, sometimes too much, and many women, untrained and unemployable at any decent job, need it. Prostitution is an economic problem, although it involves personal and social disasters as a direct result of the way it currently operates.

It is ironical that prostitution as such is not illegal. If it were, both parties involved could be prosecuted, and who ever heard of the clients being fined or jailed for their role in prostitution? The system is set up so that it is the activities of the woman involved, necessary to get customers, which are illegal. Advertising for prostitution is illegal. Standing on the street waiting for customers is illegal. Any relationship with anyone else who might provide customers, protection in case of assault, or even badly-needed personal friendship and love – all these are illegal.

If a man propositions a woman for prostitution, however threatening or upsetting this is to members of the general public, he can be virtually certain that no action will be taken against him by the police, no matter how many complaints are made and despite the fact that identification and evidence are often very straightforward. This complete refusal by the police to enforce the basic laws of this country, which prevent any individual from annoying any other, amounts to a cynical decision of their own to allow the commonest introduction to prostitution to go unchallenged (men approach women far more often than the other way around). There is no need for a special law against soliciting, but the men in Parliament have seen fit to pass such a law – to apply to women only. So heinous is this supposed crime, when it is committed by women, that it carries with it a unique penalty in the form of official labelling as 'common prostitute'. The law is often applied in the most casual way, usually on the word of one policeman against the accused woman. Obviously this gives enormous power to the men in the police to blackmail prostitutes, and many cases have been reported where they threaten to 'turn her in' unless she provides sexual services for free, or pays them off in cash. Such corruption of our police force can do nothing but harm in terms of their efficiency and integrity in dealing with real criminals, who will obviously be the first to offer money and other favours to the police in return for immunity from the law.

The large fines imposed on women for soliciting have one effect only: to keep them in prostitution as the only way they can raise money for the fines and so avoid going to prison. The vilification as 'common prostitute' has a similar effect, but one lasting for a lifetime. The label can never be removed, and will be brought out constantly to prevent the woman from getting any other job, decent housing, social security as an emergency survival measure in coming off 'the game' and, worst of all, it will often be used to take her children away. This is an act of extreme cruelty to the many women who work as prostitutes in order to feed those children.

The best and simplest change in public policy, which is being strongly argued by the English Collective of Prostitutes and others, is the repeal of laws against soliciting and other prostitution-related offences. This 'decriminalisation' would not only be a matter of simple justice, but it would remove much of the reason for street soliciting and sex establishments. Prostitution would be arranged mainly by advertising; the prostitutes would have a free choice as to how they operated according to what was safest, and live with whoever they chose. The basis of the many protection

120

rackets, by petty criminals and by the police, would be removed. With no record as a 'common prostitute', the women involved would find it much easier to quit. There would also be less pressure on them to accept any client, and they would be able to organise their own lives and set their own rules as to what is, and is not, acceptable to them. Far too often prostitutes are raped, beaten up, robbed, injured and even killed without the least prospect of getting help from the law – police are more likely to laugh at a prostitute's complaint than to provide the protection of the law, and they may even arrest her when she reports an assault. Perhaps most important of all, prostitutes would no longer be censored by the constant threat of court action if they admit to working in this way. They would be able to talk about the whole business from their own point of view, for a change. They would be able to organise more freely, and to put forward their own feelings and needs as a vital contribution to any final policy that would aim to reduce the demand for commercial sex and to reduce the pressures on women, especially very young women, which force them on to the game in the first place and then make it very hard for them to leave.

Pornography: the propaganda of sexual assault?

Pornography: some would say it is better not to know. Perhaps what you do not see cannot hurt you: the lies, the cruelty, the abuse of women in pornography. Andrea Dworkin, who studied it in detail, describes the experience:

A hatred of women that literally knows no bounds has put me beyond anger and beyond tears; I can only speak to you from grief.

Together with other women who watched the films and read the magazines:

We are simply overwhelmed by the male hatred of our kind, its morbidity, its compulsiveness, its obsessiveness . . .

The essence of pornography is 'the eroticisation of murder'. It is the process of dehumanising women, tying us up, threatening and terrifying us, and committing violence of all kinds against us. This process is promoted as the most exciting sexual experience that men can have. Andrea Dworkin has managed to put into words the feelings of revulsion which many women have when we come into contact with the pornographic image of women – whether it is 'tits and bums' in the newsagents, advertisements showing us as the objects of violence, or a copy of *Playboy* or the *Sun*.

In porn, constant repetition instils into the male user the idea that women are objects, without feelings. In pornographic fantasy, what we say can be safely ignored. Our resistance to violence must be overcome, because in this fantasy world it inevitably turns into willing consent. However gruesome the injuries, porn teaches that women enjoy being raped and assaulted. In fact, in the porn version of reality women love pain. We beg men for it, and even inflict it on ourselves. A common pornographic picture, for example, will show a women exposing herself, thrusting a sharp knife up her vagina – and smiling.

These images of pain, mutilation and degradation, grotesquely accompanied by toothy grins from the models and descriptions of their supposed pleasure, are a clear invitation to the male reader to imitate the assault free of any guilt. As we know, the increasing proliferation of pornography and its invasion of advertising have been matched by increasing sexual assaults, 'domestic' violence on women who cannot get away, and rape with violence. The atrocities of Peter Sutcliffe, the so-called 'Yorkshire Ripper', are very similar to those portrayed in pornographic media.

Pornography is used by men and boys for masturbation. This powerfully reinforces the association for them between their own sexual arousal and the sexual degradation of women. 'Masturbatory conditioning', as the psychologists would describe it, means that our humiliation is necessary for their pleasure – and it is only their sensations that count. The use of pornography has been shown to create an erotic response to violence and abuse of women. It can also work to condition women's sexual response, which is why there are some women who will defend porn as a necessary sex aid. One researcher, Victor Cline, who surveyed a variety of studies on the subject, has concluded that pornographic materials 'have great potential power to assist in the shift of sexual orientation'.

This conditioning by pornography explains the phenomenon of the growing unresponsiveness to so-called 'soft' porn of many men, who demand increasingly violent and crude images for their sexual stimulation. It is not only a question of progressing from *Playboy* to the sleazier porn shops, although this happens, because the 'harder' porn is being matched by the 'acceptable' face of the trade becoming steadily more violent as time goes on. Particularly strong stimulation is obtained from pictures, films and videos. They offer virtually unlimited images progressing from group sex to bondage, enslavement, mutilation, a wide range of child abuse, and even the infamous 'snuff' films showing real murders of women. It is the video trade which is booming at the moment.

Far from providing sexual 'release' as an alternative to real-life assaults, porn incites men to crime. A vice officer writing about the trade, has commented: 'Men look at the stuff and get worked up and when they come out of the movie or nudie bar they look for a woman.' In Washington DC, crimes increased markedly in an area with the greatest number of pornography shops, while it was also dropping sharply in an area where these were closing down. In San Diego, within two weeks of the opening of a hard-core porn cinema women working night shifts nearby were repeatedly harassed, molested and sexually assaulted. Any woman who has walked through Soho or similar areas at night, even with friends, knows what the effect of porn is on some of the men in the street.

We are all involved in this business since it is providing powerful messages about all women, but there are also many direct victims of the industry. Children are being bought and sold for pornographic modelling, as well as the closely related prostitution. Many of the women in the business start because they have no other job prospects at all, and often a history of abuse as children which makes it hard for them to build up self-esteem except in a sick way as objects of abuse. To begin with they are given relatively harmless assignments since there is a premium on their young-looking faces and bodies. As they become better known, they are often forced into increasingly vicious ones which can extend to full-blown torture.

Pornography and the mass market

One thing that many women find hard to understand is the numbers of men who use porn. Especially in all-male environments, it is all over the place; it is passed around in schools to pre-pubescent boys with no real understanding of their sexuality. The armed forces are major users of violent porn, which serves to stimulate hatred of the enemy and impulses towards violence. Increasingly though, porn is being used throughout society, not just out of sight of women as it used to be. The commercial interests involved are now very big business concerns, its image has become glossy and glamorous, and men have much less need to hide it from women. The more we hesitate about the issue, the more open this sexual propaganda becomes. Especially with the phenomenal growth in video porn, the feeble legislation against 'obscenity' is proving virtually useless – laws which were drafted for printed materials are hard to apply to the new technology. The few police attempts to prosecute distributors of violent and degrading videotapes have usually been thrown out of court. One porn film, which was refused a certificate for cinema viewing, has been reported as the second-biggest selling videotape in Britain, a close second to *The Sound of Music*. The police report that there is growing involvement by organised crime in the production and distribution of porn tapes, and that profits from their booming sales are going into other criminal activities such as drug dealing.

Porn is also used increasingly to sell other products. Sexual abuse is commercial – and aimed at women as well as men. You are all prostitutes now, the hoardings tell us. You wear underclothes or eat chocolates in a way which advertises your sexual availability to all. If you do not match up to the glossy 'pro' image, if you are not young or pretty enough to be wanted, you are invisible in this world of advertising.

Sexual assaults on women are increasingly being used now to sell newspapers. It is common in some 'family' newspapers to set the page three picture of a woman with simpering smile next to a sensational story about a woman being assaulted, raped or murdered. A study summarised in a *New Society* article has shown that the pornographic reporting of rape – emphasising the woman's appearance, sexual history and the details of exactly what was done to her – has increased dramatically. Almost twice as many rapes are being reported in the press compared with a few years ago, for the titillation of their readers. Even the supposedly respectable *Times* has joined in, increasing the number of rape stories from three cases a year in 1971 to 21 in 1978, seven times the number. The *Daily Mirror*, trying to keep pace with the *Sun*, increased its coverage by three times in the same period. The lead is still held, though, by the *Sun* and the *News of the World*, which have always relied on sexual outrages to boost their sales. The main point of the story is titbits of information which seem to 'justify' the attack: the *Sun*, for example, gave a detailed account of one victim's work as a stripper. *The Times* was careful to inform us, in another case, that an 'unmarried' woman had just had a contraceptive coil fitted. The blanket coverage of the 'Ripper' trial by all the press focused mainly on which of the victims had worked as prostitutes, and the murderer's alleged divine mission against them.

Perhaps the real give-away about how the papers are using rape stories as pornography is that the *Sun* and *News of the World*, which both belong to Mr Rupert Murdoch, both make the largest use of such stories yet never report the same cases. In effect, the two are being sold as a package, with fresh descriptions in each daily *Sun* and weekly *News*. It is no wonder that women are even more reluctant to press charges for rape and sexual assault if it makes them objects of pornographic stories. Public prejudice about women 'asking for it', fed by these stories, must be having an effect on juries in rape trials. Convictions for rape fell from 34 percent in 1971 to 26 percent, barely a quarter, in 1978 when pornographic reporting of rape cases had become an epidemic.

New approaches to pornography as a women's issue

Mary Whitehouse and others have campaigned against pornography as part of their campaign against violence and against 'indecency'. More militant women, in organisations like Reclaim the Night, Women Against Violence Against Women and the Angry Women groups have marched through Soho and similar areas throughout the country. The more notorious targets have had their windows smashed, and even been set on fire. Is there room for the common elements of agreement among women to unite the two kinds of campaigns against pornography? At the moment they work in isolation from each other. The 'reactionaries' of the Mary Whitehouse campaigns are the target of vicious abuse from many men, especially in the media, who manage to portray them as the enemies of freedom (the men's freedom, that is). More militant women are also the target of a great deal of jeering from the porn users and manufacturers, and in addition have been beaten up and charged with 'assault' by the police, aided and abetted by men involved in the trade. Men of the left as well as of the right have accused us of opposing their 'free speech'.

Women's opposition can have a powerful effect, however. In one village, Ardsley in Yorkshire, women picketed a shop every day for two months after it opened near a primary school, and forced it to close; similar actions have been taking place elsewhere.

Perhaps we should emulate the American women who have made a point of recording what is going on by photographing the men who visit massage parlours and sex shops and then displaying the photos all over town. The resulting howls of outrage from the men were very gratifying. Some of them were in positions of some prestige and importance, and while they were happy to see women exposed to ridicule their sense of humour was decidedly lacking when something much milder happened to them.

Those responsible for pornographic advertisements can also feel the pressure. One of the most obnoxious of recent campaigns was for 'Lovable' women's underwear, with the message 'Underneath, they're *all* Lovable'. Pictures of an angry-looking woman, fully dressed, were inset into blow-up shots of the same woman stripped to her bra and knickers, and with a come-hither leer on her face. Officials of the London Underground, pressured by Labour Party women to remove suggestive advertisements from tube stations, admitted that they judged which were the most offensive from the number of feminist stickers they attracted. Many of the worst were simply put on the other side of the electrified tracks, to prevent women adding their own comments to these portrayals of ourselves in poses which we recognise as pornographic. Elsewhere, there have been some inventive additions to poster advertising, some of them collected in Jill Posener's book *Spray It Loud*. A more decorous way to comment is to write to the Advertising Standards Authority, which after much resistance is beginning to admit that there *may* be a consumer issue here. Now if women ran the ASA, they would have woken up to pornographic advertisements years ago.

Metropolitan and County Councils already have powers to withhold Music and Dance licences from pornographic shows, and there is now a new way for local authorities to control the business in their areas in relation to 'sex establishments' and cinemas. The 1982 Local Government Act enabled the authorities to require licences for these establishments and to determine the number of licences that would be appropriate in any area – a number which can be zero. It is interesting that many Labour Councils have taken up the new powers, as well as solidly Conservative Councils such as Westminster, and it is women of both parties who are making most of the running. The Act is still imprecise and difficult to operate and a number of legal challenges are likely. But, if the courts apply the spirit of the law, it could establish a solid basis for getting rid of porn shops and cinemas.

Whether or not the video hire shops can be made subject to the law, when it is only some of their material which is pornographic, has still to be determined.

Further initiatives will have to be taken to change the law, and they will have to be made by women at a national level. The men in Parliament have made a number of attempts over the years to tackle what they call 'indecency', a very weak concept which they have completely failed to define. The question of whether or not material is sexually explicit, as in sex education materials or information about contraceptives, is not the point – in fact there is some disagreement among women who are agreed on the need to confront the pornography business about sexually explicit materials written or produced by women for women. If there is any attempt to legislate against 'indecency' which includes the sort of material produced by women to combat our own ignorance about our bodies and sexuality, then it will be strongly resisted. The issue on which women agree is the false propaganda spread by some men about us and our sexuality: in a word, pornography. The word is derived from the Greek for 'prostitute' and 'picture'. Porn depicts all women as prostitutes. And a prostitute is fair game for any kind of abuse in order to give the men a thrill.

If we are to fight it we shall have to change the whole approach quite radically, away from the men's self-centred definitions. An excellent example of how not to challenge porn was the Private Member's Bill introduced by the Conservative MP, Tim Sainsbury. This, now the Indecent Displays (Control) Act, was intended to remove 'indecent' material from public display; it does nothing about the actual use of the material. When the Second Reading was moved virtually all the MPs speaking to it were men who talked only of their own embarrassment, and that of other men, at seeing pornography on display. Liberal MP Clement Freud summed up the men's attitude:

It is a disgrace that there are streets in Britain where you cannot take a friend, or a child or a sensitive wife without substantial chance of embarrassment. It is a misery you cannot take your grandson into a newsagent for fear he will find the pornography before the Smarties.

Shirley Summerskill, who should know better, described 'indecency' in the words of a male judge as 'something that offends the modesty of the average man'. This concern with the purity and

127

modesty of men is very touching, but completely misses the point about pornography which is its portrayal of women. The porn industry has had no real worries about the new Act since it not only makes no mention of the actual use of pornography, but does not even attempt to define the 'indecency' which it seeks to remove from public view.

A radically new approach to the issue, and one which has just been introduced in France under very strong pressure from the women's movement, would be to legislate for women to be able to bring our own case against the pornographers by means of an action for defamation. At the moment, all that our libel laws do is to act as a powerful form of censorship on journalists who are seeking to expose the corrupt activities of powerful individuals. It would be much more socially useful if libel actions could be undertaken without having a small fortune available to pay the costs. Legal aid should be made available for defamation cases, and it should be possible to bring a 'class action' on behalf of the group of people being slandered. In the case of pornography this could mean any group of women. The concept would also be a very useful one for other groups subject to violent abuse and assaults: Jews in the case of pro-Nazi literature, and racial minorities in the case of much of the propaganda being put out by the National Front and similar groups. It could also apply to lesbians, and gay men. Race relations legislation has proved very disappointing as a way of getting rid of racist propaganda since the police and the Director of Public Prosecutions have been unwilling to act. A new approach which brought any kind of defamation or incitement to assault into the law of libel could prove something of a breakthrough.

A new approach to pornography, as a women's, not a men's issue, is long overdue. A Gallup survey in 1979 showed that a large majority of people were opposed to the business, particularly among older people. Women were more likely to be opposed than men, and almost two thirds of those surveyed agreed with the idea that porn degrades women by making us into sex objects for abuse by men.

Pornography carries the message that women are less than human. Men can take no notice of what we say – we do not really mean it. We have no valid needs of our own. If we are hurt, our pain is not real. Men's contempt for women as shown in pornography bears an uncanny resemblance to their contempt for us in politics, their disregard for our interests and opinions and their failure to understand what we say. Porn could be the first instance where women get together politically to reclaim an issue as ours. Perhaps if we can find a way to challenge the pornographic view of women and our place in the world, we can make our voice heard politically on other issues as well.

Resources

Two books are available which provide an insight into prostitution as seen by the women working in it: *Prostitutes: our life*, edited by Claude Jaget (Falling Wall Press, 1980); and *Women Working: Prostitution now*, by Eileen McLeod (Croom Helm, 1982).

For an insight into the reality for women that lies behind the apparent glamour of the sex industry read the story of 'Linda Lovelace', the most famous porn star ever, in *Ordeal: An autobiography* (Star Paperbacks, London, 1980).

The English Collective of Prostitutes is based at King's Cross Women's Centre, 71 Tonbridge Street, London WC1. It is campaigning for the decriminalisation of women's activities related to prostitution, and also acting as a research and advice centre for prostitutes and those interested in their problems.

Women Against Violence Against Women (WAVAW) has been active on a number of issues involving the sex industry, and has organised against pornography in particular. They, together with Reclaim the Night and other groups, can be contacted via A Woman's Place, Hungerford House, Victoria Embankment, London WC2 (tel: 01-930 1584).

There are two recent books on pornography, both published in 1981 by The Women's Press: Susan Griffin's *Pornography and Silence*, and Andrea Dworkin's *Pornography: Men possessing women*. Jill Posener's *Spray It Loud* was published by Routledge and Kegan Paul, London, in 1982. The article in *New Society* mentioned in this chapter is by Alex Hau, Keith Soothill and Sylvia Walby, 'Seducing the public by rape reports', in the issue of 31 July 1980.

To complain about pornographic advertising, write to the Advertising Standards Authority at Brook House, Torrington Place, London WC1.

10
Feeling Safe?

One of the most important issues for many people is that labelled 'law and order', as if the law, as it stands, ensures public order. Perhaps, to many of the learned gentlemen who run our legal system, questions about the law amount only to the problem of enforcement, catching the law-breakers, and which punishment can be imposed for which crime. 'Law and order' is often portrayed in terms of the death sentence for murder, or corporal punishment for young offenders involved in vandalism, street robberies and petty crime in general. For women, though, much of the debate about 'law and order' misses the central point: that the law itself is out of order. It makes no attempt to provide a real deterrent to assaults on women, the great majority of which are dismissed as (provoked?) rape, sexual assault or 'domestic disputes'. Even in cases of the most brutal murders of women and girls, the law often works against the victim.

Looking at the criminal law, it is no use giving all our attention to Parliament and its legislation. There is a vast body of 'case law', based on milestone decisions of the higher courts and the House of Lords, which is at least as important as the legislation. Related to this, also, is the all-male character of the judges and almost all the barristers arguing cases in court.

Until very recently, juries were also made up of men only. The legal world is extremely conservative, as are many judges and other lawyers; many of the landmark decisions used to decide on cases of assault on women were taken in the time when women were seen as the property of their husbands or fathers. We should not be surprised at the courts' failure to tackle seriously the kidnapping, vicious attacks, rape and sometimes murder of women, since they have *always* reacted in this way in cases where women were the victims. 'Leaders' of public opinion, those in control of the media, have applauded the decisions.

In case this seems an exaggeration, consider just a few of the

130

cases to come before the courts recently. In 1980 a man who was convicted of raping a seven-year-old girl 17 times was freed by the court, on the grounds that the interests of society would not be served by sending him to prison. No evidence was offered that he would not make further attacks. In 1981, the case of PC Swindell came before the courts, accused of murdering a woman he had picked up for prostitution. Swindell admitted that the woman had died in his house, that he had dismembered her body and disposed of it secretly, and that he had used a rubber mask over her face which would severely constrict her breathing. Yet the prosecution did not pursue the question of how she had been killed, and by whom. Swindell went free. At about the same time, Beatrix Rutherford was killed by two men who had moved into her flat on the pretext of 'helping' her. In their defence the two claimed to have been possessed by the devil and carrying out an 'exorcism', but made no plea of insanity. The judge, in sentencing them to a very brief prison term, described them as 'two upright Christian men who acted out of misguided motives and not maliciously'. The press made much of the victim's broken relationship with another woman, which had led her to accept 'help' from the men. This was yet another case of 'blame the victim', in her case for being a lesbian, and in the Swindell case working as a prostitute.

A woman with 25 years' experience as a magistrate in a busy city court, Thelma Kellgren, wrote to the *Guardian*:

> The violent acts of men against women and children are frequent, dreadful and often inexplicable . . . In the meantime we must feel *safe*.

She cited the verdict of not guilty on PC Swindell as making it impossible for any woman to feel safe:

> I want protection for myself, my daughters, my granddaughters and every girl and woman in England at this moment. I want to feel complete confidence in the law and its interpretation . . . There are too many questions with unsatisfactory answers.

There is in fact a consistent pattern of murder and serious assault cases where male criminals are given very light sentences, or acquitted, on the grounds that the victim in some way deserved the crime committed against her. By far the worst of these is the case of the so-called 'Yorkshire Ripper', Peter Sutcliffe, whose victims included many women working as prostitutes. It was not until quite a late stage in the series of murders and attempted murders, when the police announced that the victim was not a prostitute, that the legal authorities showed particular concern. Women throughout West Yorkshire and beyond were terrorised by the vicious murders: after every attack, women would stay at home after dark, and there would be a sudden slump in demand for evening entertainment. There was a run on second-hand cars as women sought ways of avoiding men in the streets. When Sutcliffe was finally caught, there was a sense of guarded relief – an awareness that although this particular killer had been tracked down, the details of the murders had been well publicised, and many men had taken a lascivious interest in them. The man who was supposed to be leading the prosecution for the Crown, Michael Havers, astonished the court on the opening day of the trial by making a speech on Sutcliffe's 'divine mission' against prostitutes which would have served quite adequately as the defence, and in fact this was Sutcliffe's defence, although he had produced this 'mission' at a very late stage in the police interrogation. Such a mission has been claimed by many of the men who have committed multiple murders against women and girls, often with an element of torture involved, and this pretext is frequently accepted regardless of whether the victims are working as prostitutes or not. The press had a field day dissecting the reputations of many of Sutcliffe's victims. His wife, too, was viciously attacked both inside and outside the court and accused of being naive, self-centred and domineering. By the end of the trial, the press if not the court had convinced itself that Sutcliffe was really the innocent victim of evil women, not the other way around.

I have emphasised the law's attitude towards serious crimes by men against women and girls because this is also the pattern for the petty assault, harassment and verbal abuse which is or has been the experience of all women. It is directed particularly at adolescent girls, who are vulnerable to the embarrassment, humiliation and appalling frustration that these men seek to induce; it remains buried deep inside a mature woman's mind even though she tries to repress the memory of those incidents where men whisper obscenities in her ear, touch her on the streets, follow her, expose themselves to her in dark and lonely corners, or rub against her in a crowded train or elsewhere, making her want to scream, while nobody notices and she is too ashamed to do or say anything. We learn to avoid the worst situations where these minor assaults can happen, but at the price of constant vigilance. There is the memory of abuse, the constant reminder in the obscene comments, and the threat that some day, a serious assault or rape could happen to you. When it does, you probably will not report it just as you did not report the flashers or touchers when you were a teenager.

One of the great ironies about the failure of our legal system to investigate or seriously deter assaults on women – major or minor – is that any attempt to relieve women of fear would be so easy to do. The police could have a high detection rate in crimes of rape and assault, just from the fact that so many of the attackers are actually known to their victims. In the case of men soliciting or flashing at girls and women from cars, it is a simple matter of taking the car number. In cases of domestic violence against women, where the police are notoriously unwilling to help the victim, it is perfectly obvious who is committing the assault. In many cases there is already a court injunction on the man involved not to assault the woman – an injunction which the police often refuse to enforce unless it has a 'power of arrest' attached. This is a condition which applies to no other kind of injunction: the police are required to enforce these automatically. The police frequently plead lack of 'manpower' or difficulties in detecting forms of crime where there is public criticism of their role. This can hardly be a valid excuse in terms of their persistent failure to act in cases of assaults on women. If there were genuine community control of the police, through local government or other means, women would have the chance to argue the case for enforcing the law against assaults on us. As things stand at present, the police take their lead from the virtually all-male judiciary, and are legally accountable to no one except whichever man is Home Secretary at the time.

The crime of rape

A journalist, Jean Stead, has suggested that women who are assaulted will never get justice until the crime of rape has been abandoned: a drastic view, but one which reflects the failure of the police and courts to enforce the rape laws on women's behalf. The police and courts frequently disbelieve the victim's account of the assault, something which virtually never happens in any other category of crime. Some rapes are legal – if they are committed by a woman's husband. There is frequently an interrogation of the victim herself which portrays her as a criminal. Her treatment by the police and the fact of being forced to appear in court to be cross-examined on the whole incident – again, something to which victims are not exposed in any other category of crime – is experienced by many victims as a second rape, also by men, but this time in public and in cold blood.

Jean Stead pointed out in a *Guardian* article that rape often involves a whole range of assaults: wounding, kidnap, grievous bodily harm or assault with intent to rob, which are serious offences in the eyes of the law. Yet many rape victims with horrific injuries are being asked to prove that there was penile penetration and that they were not willing accomplices of the crimes against them. If the 'rape' cannot be proved by the victim in this way, all the other assaults are automatically disregarded by the law. To add insult to injury, many judges are ignoring the recent legislation which discourages cross-examination of the victim about her previous sexual history and relationship with the accused. The distinctions made are such as to take rape victims outside the protection of normal legal procedures: the courts do not ask the victims of common assault, for example, whether or not they were willing to be struck. The fact of injury is regarded as clear proof of the assault having taken place.

In a recent notorious case in Scotland, where a woman had been repeatedly slashed with knives while she was unconscious, the judge commented that if a woman was virtually insensible it would not be rape to have intercourse with her – and the slashing was regarded as part of the rape. It took a rare private prosecution to put the attackers in jail. An even more outrageous comment was made by Judge Bertrand Richards, who raised a storm of anger among women when he accused one victim of rape of 'contributory negligence', a concept which does not exist in criminal law. Lord Hailsham, the Lord Chancellor at the time, had himself infuriated many women in a 1975 House of Lords appeal, when he accepted the suggestion that self-defence by a rape victim might reasonably be seen by the attacker as being provided for 'the additional thrill of the struggle'.

The approach suggested by Jean Stead of trying rape cases as assault cases has much to commend it, since the use of violence which is at the heart of the crime of rape might then be dealt with by barristers and judges in the same way as any other form of violence. It leaves open, of course, the question of the sexual offence as such – but here too the present law is of very little value.

Forced penetration by a man's penis is seen as rape, but not the much worse phenomenon, all too common, of penetration by a variety of objects which can include broken bottles and other weapons. There is also the whole question of forced sexual acts which are disgusting, humiliating and often very painful to the women concerned, but do not involve penetration. And last but not least, there is the coercion of sexual acts by means of threats, intimidation, deception, blackmail and so on which the law at present sees as involving 'consent'. There is an urgent need for sexual assault to be seen as the violence which it is (rape has little to do with sexual impulses), and for the use of coercion for any sexual activity to be made the subject of wide-ranging legislative reform.

Some drastic action is needed to deter sexual assault, since it is such a common and yet unreported crime and has such a devastating effect on the victims as well as intimidating women in general; all of us are potential victims. The effects of a violent or forced sexual encounter, against the will of the woman concerned, are traumatic. The motive is to punish or humiliate her, the exact opposite of true sexual intimacy, and is seen by many campaigners on the issue as a means by which men control and intimidate women. Men who commit rape are not some special category of men, and are certainly not over-sexed as the male myths and jokes would have it. They have a 'normal' male hostility towards women, and act this out through abusing our sexuality.

Rape and sexual abuse are very common elements in torture all over the world. The files of Amnesty International are full of evidence of this, where the sexual organs – of both sexes – are subjected to extreme pain, mutilation and abuse. It seems to be the ultimate in expressions of hatred and sadism, where the victim is deprived of all control even over her own body. Certainly, rape fits into the definition of 'Torture and Other Cruel, Inhuman or Degrading Treatment or Punishment' as defined in a United Nations Declaration of 1975:

> For the purpose of this Declaration, torture means any act by which severe pain and suffering, whether physical or mental, is intentionally inflicted . . . on a person for such purposes as obtaining from him [her] or a third person information or confession, punishing him [her] for an act he [she] has committed or is suspected of having committed, or intimidating him [her] or other persons.

The Declaration refers to 'public officials' as the instigators of torture, but the description fits also the more powerful groups in society and their dealings with less powerful ones – particularly women. Men exercise the power through attacking women in gangs, by assaulting women who are obviously smaller or less fit, and by the use of weapons, drugs or alcohol. They can also abuse the legal or financial powers they possess over women, for instance as employers or supervisors with the power to create difficulties at work or to get women fired.

A special category of sexual abuse is that involving men who abuse their power over children and young teenagers. The girl does what her father or other relative tells her, without knowing what it is or what it means, but anxious to keep his approval and affection and, on his instructions, keeping the whole affair completely secret. Victims of incest are often seriously disturbed, many prostitutes and drug addicts were sexually molested as children, and feel crippling guilt and self-hatred for their complicity. The one piece of law which protects girls from this is the 'Age of Consent', currently 16. In practice it is used to prosecute older men, not boys of the same age, whose experiments do not have the same traumatising effect. The girl is on a much more equal footing with someone of the same age. It was women, campaigning against prostitution in the nineteenth century, who established the Age of Consent. A recent Home Office proposal to reduce it to 14 has met strong opposition from the many women's organisations still concerned about the sexual abuse of girls.

Rape and sexual abuse may leave few obvious external marks on the victim, although there are often internal injuries. By far the most serious consequence, however, is the long-term trauma from which many of the victims never recover. In an official American study of rape victims in 1982, it was found that several years after the crime about 60 per cent of the women involved were still so traumatised that they experienced difficulties in sexual relations with men. Many also suffered from long-term fearfulness and depression. In the case of the others who had recovered, this was almost always related to sympathetic support from the authorities and from people in general. For this, it was vital that there should be no suggestion that the woman was guilty of provoking the assault. It seems clear from this that any woman who reports the crime of rape to the police and courts, under the present system of 'blame the victim', is unlikely to recover fully from the trauma of the event and its aftermath. The behaviour of male lawyers and

136

police does indeed, according to this study, amount to a 'second rape'.

The law is much weaker on the abuse of girls than when boys are the victims: sentencing patterns show a clear double standard. Men seem to have little understanding of the horror attached to sexual abuse, and the self-hatred as well as fear of future attacks which results from it. It is seen by many men as a joke, until they contemplate such a crime being committed against *them*. A popular film of a few years ago, called *Deliverance*, featured the rape of a man by another man and his friend who threatened him with a rifle. Many men identified immediately with the victim, and found the whole scene very traumatic; they identified with the feelings behind the revenge killing of the rapist. If only men could see themselves more often as the victims of rape, instead of finding ways of justifying it, women might begin to feel safer in the knowledge that we too are protected by the law.

Assault and battery

It is not just physical strength which gives violent criminals the power over their victims. Equally important is an attacker's readiness to use violence, and the reluctance of the victim to use such violence herself even under extreme provocation. Boys and men learn to fight in the school playground, at boxing clubs or in the armed forces, they get used to the idea of hurting other people physically. Women are likely to be extremely inhibited about this, and it puts us at a great disadvantage which is probably far more telling in a violent situation than physical size or strength. When a woman is subjected to violence over a long period of time, and also has a real stake in the home and family where the attacks are taking place, she can easily become more and more incapable of planning a systematic strategy for dealing with it, especially as there are no outsiders who can be relied on to support her when exposed to an attack. One detailed study found that battery victims were being officially dismissed as 'masochists' for their inability to defend themselves, but they were in fact immobilised by their 'paralyzing terror' of the violence, together with fear of their own feelings of rage and hatred towards the batterer which could reach homicidal intensity. They were afraid of what they might do if they allowed themselves to strike back. Indeed, many of the women who do murder their husbands have been through many years of battering at their hands, and suddenly give way to the violent hatred which this has evoked in them over that time.

In many cases, battery starts at a time when a woman is particularly dependent, such as when she is pregnant, ill or has small children and nowhere to go. Society in general has made it very difficult for a woman to leave her husband and home. She is often deeply ashamed of her situation, which she tries to hide from other people. Many of the families are also very isolated socially because of the husbands' intense jealousy about any outside contacts or friendships the women may have. Like rape victims who feel intense guilt and humiliation, battered women half-believe their husbands' and other men's line that it is they who are somehow responsible for their own injuries because of something bad they must have done or said to provoke the attacks.

In marriages where there is systematic violence and abuse the question should be not why the women stay, but how they can obtain protection from an attack or find a way to leave altogether. This is the crucial political issue. If it is answered adequately it should deter many of the assaults, as violent husbands will see that women and children can easily escape if they attack, or call in effective protection from the police and the courts. Under the present system, the more a woman is battered, physically and mentally, the more aggressive her husband is likely to be, since he becomes convinced that he can attack with impunity and is some kind of superior being who is above the law. Men who kill their wives have often been assaulting them over a long period of time with no attempt by the authorities to stop the mounting violence. The cycle of violence, once started, can also be taught to children, especially boys, who grow up to become violent in their turn. Girls from violent families also suffer great distress, and may mature with a lack of confidence in themselves and their rights which leaves them vulnerable to aggression and violence from others.

The amount of domestic violence is staggering, leading some to see the family itself as a violent institution as it is organised at present, with much of the income, outside contacts and general influence being given to the husband, and a 'dependent' role being the norm for a woman, her place being 'in the home' as if it were a prison, and with very little bargaining power with her husband. This is very much a matter of the law on marriage, and of the discrimination against women in the job market and elsewhere. It is particularly fierce in regard to married women, especially those with small children.

One of the worst features of assault and battery within the family is that it is so 'normal', and so widespread. One American study has estimated that 'spouse abuse' occurs in almost half of all marriages. FBI figures show it to be three times as common as rape, although both are unlikely to be reported so that there is great uncertainty about the figures. Studies of men who batter women show that they are no more likely to be mentally ill than any other men. In fact the attitudes behind the man's behaviour are those of most men: the stereotype of the 'woman's place', and the insistence on her playing the role of the docile wife all the time without a life or activities of her own. The man may have some very good qualities despite his violent behaviour, and this may make it all the harder for the woman involved to reject his promises of reform and to leave him altogether. However, like many men the typical batterer will find it very hard to be intimate with anybody, even his wife – this would involve honesty about himself as distinct from the 'he-man' image he projects. Sexually, he acts out the male jokes, treating the woman as an instrument for his satisfaction without any feelings of her own. Some battered women dread the TV programmes which show the 'tough guy' being violent to the villains, they know that their husbands will often imitate the 'hero', but that they will be the victim. Last but not least, the batterer refuses to accept personal responsibility for his behaviour, however disgusting, and invariably blames the woman for her own injuries. A very common excuse is that the woman 'nagged', a nasty word which can be applied to anything a woman says, especially a personal opinion or a complaint which the husband does not want to hear. A response to women's speech in the form of physical brutality can effectively reduce the victim to total silence. Prolonged battery, like assaults or torture of prisoners who cannot get away, does as much psychological damage as physical. The victim is forced to 'confess' her alleged crimes, or to denounce her own friends, opinions and way of life. There is a complete block imposed on her expressing her real feelings and needs. The man who batters is insecure about the artificial 'master' role which he has assumed as a husband, and cannot tolerate any expression of opinion from the woman which might contradict his – and society's – prejudices about women in general and our place in a family. This helps to explain the great increase in domestic violence which is known to be triggered by male unemployment: he is effectively reduced to *her* level and he cannot deal with the threat to his pretensions of superiority.

The answer to domestic violence is not to reinforce the man's prejudices about his 'superiority' or to accept the idea that his wife is provoking his attacks. Just as the law responds to other violent crimes by providing a severe punishment as deterrent, it needs to react with equal seriousness to any attacks which take place in the home. Society has to place strong limits on the actions of any individual which harm or intimidate others, and must challenge a man who claims that someone else, the victim, is somehow responsible for *his* violence towards her. At the same time, we must reduce and eventually eliminate the imbalance of power between men and women so that they can work out a relationship that meets both their needs, and does not allow one to become the target of the other. Some men may need help in learning to control their behaviour towards women, and to see us as human beings with rights of our own instead of the alien beings that they imagine. This re-education should be part of the rehabilitation of offenders, and of our system of bringing up boys so that they will not become violent, abusive or exploitative towards those they live with.

If the batterers' attitudes are to change, we first need almost a revolution in attitudes from the various public authorities, from the police to the medical services and the social workers employed by local authorities. A detailed study of battering by the National Women's Aid Federation (NWAF) found that women who finally reached their refuges had approached an average of *five* sources of help without getting any effective support from the official bodies. Many of the professionals involved had not even known of the NWAF refuges, although voluntary organisations were much better informed. The statutory authorities had not grasped the elementary fact that domestic violence tends to get worse if it is not challenged by outside agencies taking up the woman's complaints. They very often dismissed the reports of assault as exaggerated, although the women reaching the refuges had all suffered serious assaults over a long period of time, the average being seven years. The NWAF researchers conclude that the immediate need is for protection and somewhere to go to escape the violence. The agencies with most power to act – the police and the local authorities' housing departments – had in fact been the least helpful to women complaining of battering. Of the social workers, only one in a hundred reacted by challenging the violence. The others tried by various means to 'reconcile' the couple or dismissed the assaults as unimportant.

There is so much that could easily be done by the official agencies. Doctors, social workers, housing officials and the police could be told the facts about domestic violence, and the legal protection which is available. Instead of trying to force women and children back into violent homes, the professionals should either intervene to halt the violence, or help the victims to get away. The police in Newcastle have installed alarms in the homes of women and children whose husbands and fathers have been served an injunction by the courts, so that victims can call for immediate police help if the husbands attack. Police, everywhere, who are very often called into domestic violence cases, should have a standard procedure for removing the violent person and investigating the assault just as they would if it had happened on the street. Prosecutions could hardly be simpler, since there is usually no question about who committed the assault. In fact the clear-up rate on violent crime, which at present looks decidedly poor for the police, would be greatly improved by bringing cases against domestic batterers for assault, grievous bodily harm or any of the other relevant offences. It is estimated that domestic assaults account for at least a quarter of all violent crime, a large proportion which the police should take very seriously. It is much more important and threatening than the minor street assaults and robberies that go under the name of 'mugging', which the press and politicians have made into such a big issue.

It is not just the law which needs to be changed to deal with domestic assaults: criminal law already provides harsh penalties for violence or even threats of violence. It is the application of the law which is the problem, and especially the failure of the police and courts to apply it to violence in the home. More often than not, when they are called in the police do not take notes of the injuries

141

caused and eye-witness reports of what has happened; instead they will try to persuade the woman concerned not to make a formal complaint, after she has called them in for protection. They have been known to joke with the attacker about his crime, and give every sign of approval – or at least of understanding and sympathy for his version of events, which he will interpret as encouragement for further attacks.

At the moment, because of the failure of the criminal law in these cases, there have to be special provisions to allow the victims to bring civil cases to stop the attackers from making further assaults. Such an approach to violent street crime would be absolutely unthinkable. In 1976 Parliament passed the Domestic Violence and Matrimonial Proceedings Act to allow judges in the County Court to order husbands to stop assaulting their wives or lovers. The Act fails to deal with the considerable number of men who attack other female relatives. There is a rather meaningless 'non-molestation order' and the more difficult exclusion order, which can exclude a violent man from the home. There is absolute discretion as to whether there is a 'power of arrest' attached to either order, so some judges use this regularly and others never, regardless of how serious the injuries are. The police then fail, in many cases, to take any action against a man who ignores an injunction without the power of arrest attached, and in some cases they even disregard one which has this power. Many police officers seem to be ignorant of its meaning. The courts are limiting their own jurisdiction: in 1979, for example, only a third of the domestic violence injunctions had the power of arrest. The Home Office, meanwhile, has issued guidance to them – against the intentions of the law – to restrict those powers to only three months. In addition, there is a tendency to apply the exclusion order to only one part of the house or flat, suggesting that assaults are not allowed in the bedroom but are quite all right in the kitchen. The law is so inconsistent and inadequate that it is not surprising to find that the police themselves prefer to make arrests for the offence of Actual Bodily Harm rather than for breaches of the Domestic Violence Act, which has in fact led to very few arrests even in cases of the most sickening brutality. The Act has also failed to deal with issues commonly arising out of domestic violence, such as proceedings for taking children into care, maintenance of dependants and the division of jointly owned property.

Perhaps the only real advance for women suffering repeated

142

assaults in their own homes is the establishment of a network of refuges, nearly all of them run by Women's Aid groups on a largely voluntary basis. Most are run on a shoestring, grotesquely overcrowded with the women and their children who will put up with any conditions in order to escape the violence at home. It is widely accepted that the refuges are dealing with 'the tip of the iceberg' and it is obvious that there is a great need for more of them since they fill up as soon as they are opened, become overcrowded and even have to turn women and children away. Many areas of the country have no refuges at all. There is a very urgent need for local authorities to support the establishment of more and better equipped refuges as an emergency rescue operation. Many changes are also needed in terms of allocation of council housing to enable the women to keep the family home or, as they often prefer, to move somewhere new with their children where they can feel safe.

There is no substitute though for a complete change in the way the law is applied in dealing with all assaults, whether they take place in the street or in a home, by a stranger or a member of one's family. A double standard seems to operate throughout the criminal justice system, from the top judges and Law Lords right down to the humble police officer – and certainly in the Home Office – which actually condones many of the worst assaults on women or provides for only the mildest and most inconsistent application of a deterrent. There is a theme of 'blame the victim' running throughout the handling of cases which is being applied almost exclusively to women, whether as victims of rape and sexual abuse, systematic violence at home, or harassment in daily life. The police and the courts must be made properly accountable to women, and criminal law applied whether the victim is a woman or a man.

Until that happens, we shall not be able to feel safe. And to live under the constant threat of violence is to live without real freedom.

Resources

Rape Crisis Centres have been set up in a number of towns and cities, usually with an unlisted address in order to provide a safe place for rape victims to go for counselling. Many of those who receive help are suffering from assaults which took place some time ago. Help is also provided on an emergency basis wherever possible, and there is no pressure to report the crime to the police.

The telephone number can be found in the directory, or in some places the operator will make a direct connection.

Women's Aid groups operate on a similar basis, providing refuges whose addresses are not publicised and advising on how to deal with the courts, housing authorities, social security and the rest. Most of the groups are affiliated to the National Women's Aid Federations of England, Scotland, Wales and Northern Ireland.

Leaving Violent Men: A study of refuges and housing for battered women is the best study available for this country on the subject. It was carried out by the Women's Aid Federation England on behalf of the Department of the Environment and published in 1981 by the Federation (address page 105), price £2.

Miriam F. Hirsch, *Women and Violence* (Van Nostrand Reinhold, New York, 1981) has chapters on all the issues discussed here plus some more, and a particularly good one on the latest American research on battering.

Jean Stead's article was in the *Guardian* of 28 June 1982.

144

11
Getting Older

Women past the mid-point in life, 35 or 40, represent the key to mobilising women as a strong political force. We are often much freer, better organised and more experienced than our younger sisters. We hold together not only the women's organisations but also a vast range of campaigns, pressure groups and political bodies, especially at the local level, which simply could not operate without our skills and commitment. We are at the centre of much political life in this country, whether it is party-political or concerned with a particular issue from a non-partisan position. Yet we remain largely unrecognised by the politicians as well as greatly undervaluing ourselves. Just as society as a whole attaches little importance to a woman past child-bearing age, older women are undermined by a lack of self-esteem and a feeling of being considered by the rest of the world to be useless.

Women in the forties and fifties often experience a surge of energy and a feeling of liberation from the routine domestic world, just at the time when men of similar age are slowing down and perhaps retreating back into the cosy private sphere of the family. The result can often be problems within the marriage, and conflict with teenage or young adult children who may be the last to support their mother's liberation from the family commitments. There will often be major new responsibilities for elderly parents or other relatives, including the husband's, which impose a perhaps crippling burden of physical and emotional responsibility. Women in mid-life (or middle-age if you prefer the more humdrum expression) are very much involved in the problems of the elderly, and in fact could be considered experts on the subject. The whole question of community and other support for dependent elderly people is one of decisive importance for the women who are taking the main responsibility for looking after them. Any cut-backs in hospital, residential or home services for the elderly has an immediate impact on the women of the next generation. The catch-phrase is 'care in the community', but the reality is dumping the problem on the nearest available woman in the family without the nursing help, the respite care for days off or holidays, the day-care centres, home helps, laundry service, meals on wheels or any of the other services which can make it possible to care for the ill person in the community. The Conservative Government's reductions in the Health Service and in the rate support grant to local authorities have eliminated vital support services just when they are most needed.

If we could get the resources necessary to keep pensioners self-sufficient, many women in 'mid-life' would be liberated to an extent that far exceeds even the liberation of younger women which has been the biggest achievement of the women's movement so far. Women with frail or disabled parents or other relatives need to have a real choice about how much time they will give to looking after them. At the moment it is a question of an almost full-time commitment, overriding any other interests and outside involvement.

There has recently been a considerable growth of interest in and research into the problems and prospects of women in 'mid-life', and it is apparent that here is an enormous amount of wasted talent, energy and organisational capacity. Depression, low self-esteem, and both mental and physical illness increase markedly in the 40s and 50s. Until recently this was popularly believed to be the result of the 'change of life' or menopause, although it is becoming clear that this physical change is of little importance compared with the social and family stresses imposed on women as we get older. Women in paid employment – and the typical employed woman is now an older married woman rather than the young single – are often in boring jobs with no prospects. Those without jobs suffer badly from the increasing contempt for the 'housewife' and especially for the 'middle-class woman' so despised by the young men of the left. Their voluntary work is becoming increasingly difficult as the need for help increases, especially from the elderly, and the number of women with any spare time dwindles. The unpaid community work of the future will increasingly have to be done by retired people. Those who are able to commit time to it will have to be given more recognition and support by the community as a whole, in terms of money and training.

Older women have great problems, but they also have great potential which is not being realised at present. All women should be organising politically, whether through political parties or single-issue campaigns, to improve conditions for the women over 40. If it is not our present reality, then it is obviously our future. 'Community care' must be supported by a massive increase in community services and facilities. Training courses must be opened up to mature women, job prospects improved, the age barrier to starting new jobs eliminated, and older men encouraged to share women's responsibilities in the family and community. Perhaps the most vital element in such a change would be breaking down the mutual hostility that too often exists between older and younger women, employed and 'housewife', right-on and fuddy-duddy.

A further extension of this would have to be an interest throughout the women's movement in the problems and prospects of old age. Not only is this relevant to us personally, but old age is already a women's issue since the great majority of pensioners are women, and their problems are even worse than those of the men. Women looking after old people cannot be truly liberated until our own mothers and grandmothers are – liberated from ill-health, from loneliness, from a feeling of being useless and dependent, and from the imprisonment of being unable to leave the house. Above all, liberated from the crippling poverty of a woman's pension.

Poverty

By far the biggest issue associated with aging is retirement: the age of retirement, and the pension that goes with it. Much effort has been expended in the EOC and elsewhere, aimed at bringing the retirement age for men (now 65) and women (now 60) into line. This certainly shows a recognition of the importance of older women and their pensions, but the argument has been a complicated one that perhaps ignores the most important question about the age of retirement for both women and men: why should anybody be forced to retire at some arbitrary age which may bear no relation to the real needs and interests of the person concerned? Why should certain people like doctors and judges be completely exempt from the fixed retirement age, while others are not? Why not a retirement age *range* which would allow early or late retirement, or possibly a transition to part-time work before stopping altogether? This is already an important demand of the American 'Grey Panthers' and other pressure groups of retired people. If a choice becomes possible, then women and men could

147

enjoy real equality while preserving personal freedom and flexibility. A married couple might very often prefer to retire at the same time, for example. Or a woman who started a new career after her children had grown up, and was both fit and anxious to take on a fairly long period of responsibility in her job, may well want to retire much later than a man who had already had a very long working life by the age of 55 or 60. There would be less wastage of the training invested in mature students (most of them women) and less discrimination against women by the imposition of age barriers for starting many jobs (especially in the Civil Service and other big institutions) if the early retirement age of 60 for women could be waived.

With more freedom of choice, retirement would become less traumatic for all concerned and more a matter of planning and choice. A number of employers are now providing courses in planning for retirement, mainly for men – but ignoring the perhaps worse effects of mandatory retirement on the women they employ, and showing even less concern about the effect on a male employee's wife if she is already at home. The sudden invasion of her own personal sphere by a perhaps frustrated and demanding husband can often be a great shock to a woman at retirement. It need hardly be said that women are not really allowed to retire: they continue to do many hours of housework a day until they drop dead, even though this can become a great effort. Greater equality at work and in the home, from an earlier stage, would greatly ease the tensions that arise from having a retired husband at home who will not start to do his share of the domestic work.

The worst problems, though, are usually the financial ones. To put it mildly, living on most retirement or widows' pensions is living in poverty. Like most poverty, this too is mainly a problem for women. We get much worse pension rights because of the insecurity of our jobs, and the low pay and therefore poor fringe benefits that go with it. Not many women participate in company pension schemes, and we do not have the long years of unbroken employment which give the best deal from these schemes. Even National Insurance has been applied to married women, until very recently, at lower levels of both payments and benefits. Many women are dependent first on their husbands' earnings, then their pension, and finally the widow's pension or benefit that they get after his death, which is usually before their own because men generally die younger than women, and convention has also dictated that women should be younger than their husbands to start off with. This, together with the lower retirement age for women, has meant that the great majority of people living on a retirement pension or benefits are women. The older the age group, the more women there are compared with men.

Pensions are very often too low for the person involved to eat properly, to keep warm and comfortable, and to enjoy a normal social life – let alone to develop new interests and new capacities. No wonder that we call older women 'poor old things' and perceive them as a burden on society with their poor health and worse morale. It is ironic that the leaders of our political parties, especially the men, refuse to accept the normal retirement age for themselves, and often achieve high office at an age when many of their sisters have been consigned to a dreary 'old age' without responsibilities or power. If women in their sixties and seventies were also political leaders, perhaps policies on retirement and pensions would look very different from the way they are now. The politics and economics of old age would be recognised, at last, as the women's issues they are.

A life worth living

It makes sense for the whole community to develop a more positive policy on services for retired people. Our present mean, do-nothing approach results in massive demands being created unnecessarily on the expensive emergency services, hospital beds and many other health facilities which are not being efficiently used. There is also a huge 'opportunity cost' to the women who look after old relatives full-time, as well as the loss of a valuable contribution that fit old people can make to society through voluntary work and self-help among themselves. Poverty, malnutrition and preventable ill-health and disability have produced a growing number of dependants, since the one service our NHS will always supply is to keep people alive – if not well – wherever possible. Pneumonia, for instance, used to be a killer of old people but is now treated easily with drugs. If only our skill at preventing death could be used to make an old person's life healthier, happier and more productive, then we could truly claim to have made a long life not only technically possible, but also worth living.

The most important service is health provision. The speciality of geriatrics, which involves study of the physical changes related to aging and the different patterns of ill-health and the appropriate treatments required, will need to be given much more money and a

149

higher status in the NHS system of priorities. Geriatricians have in fact made a range of recent discoveries which make this a challenging field for medical staff, if only they have enough resources and back-up staff to make sure that specialist treatment is available as necessary. Chiropody, dentistry, dietetics, occupational therapy and a wide range of other services are particularly important to old people to remedy any physical ailments that appear, and to provide aids for the impairment of sight and hearing which affects a significant minority. Many of the services can be domiciliary or available in very localised health centres, which makes them good value for money. The expenditure on remedial health measures can also be set against the enormous expense of the emergency provision which becomes necessary if a health problem is allowed to deteriorate.

Also of vital importance to health is the provision of an adequate diet, which becomes even more important in old age. It is often left to the voluntary organisations, such as the Women's Royal Voluntary Service (WRVS), to provide the meals on wheels which are literally a lifeline to many old people. This could easily be provided on a much bigger scale by local authorities, not only by supplying people at home but also by setting up old people's lunch clubs which can often double as important centres of social and other activity as well. There are some very successful lunch clubs where people in their seventies and eighties regularly cook their own meals on a communal basis.

Many of the services most needed by the elderly are essentially practical, and at the same time not expensive to provide. Particularly for the women living alone, there is the constant problem of getting household repairs and maintenance done, especially since they were never taught to do the things their husbands took care of. Simple and very cost-effective home improvements like checking the electrical systems, putting in safety rails and other devices, and simple heat insulation can not only be a big help to old people, but a source of many new jobs for the young. A kind neighbour or relative will often help, but for many old people, especially those in the inner cities and in rural areas, there is nobody. A number of voluntary organisations try to fill the gaps, but provision is very uneven and in some places almost non-existent. There needs to be a systematic and reliable programme, funded from public revenues through local authorities, to ensure that everyone who needs practical help will be able to get it.

The same thing also applies in the area of work which is commonly left to women: housework. Many elderly women find it increasingly hard to do the basic cooking, cleaning and other jobs, and can be greatly helped by the provision of local authority 'home helps'. This has been a successful and expanding area of work, but here again the demand is much greater than the authorities can meet with their very limited Social Services funds from the Government. A national policy which involved a serious commitment to keeping old people 'in the community' would mean guaranteeing the necessary funds for home-help services to whomever could benefit from them. There are of course other groups of people other than the elderly who need such help from time to time, including women with new-born babies, disabled people and those recovering from an illness at home, and they could benefit from the existence of a substantial home-help service which was designed mainly for the elderly.

It is already widely recognised that much more specialised accommodation is needed for elderly people, to enable them to live safely and without too much strain. There is a great need for easy-to-manage housing in quiet but not isolated areas, with adequate security and a warden on call when necessary. Not only does this provide pensioners with what they need, but it also frees some of the larger accommodation they move from for rehabilitation and full occupation by others in housing need. Local authorities and housing associations have been forced to cut back sharply on old people's sheltered housing projects because of the cuts in housing allocations by the Conservative Government, and it will take years to get a programme of any size into full production. It took a big campaign to take sheltered housing out of the legislation requiring Councils and housing associations to sell their rental accommodation, and this has at least stopped the drain on specialised housing that exists, although it has forced the disposal of ground-floor flats and small maisonettes that would have been suitable for many pensioners. There will need to be a big building programme for housing old people at all levels of fitness and self-sufficiency, if their increasing numbers are not to overwhelm the available provision, as is already starting to happen in many areas.

A suitable home, and help with domestic activities, provide an important base for old people, but almost equally important is the opportunity for the occupants to keep in constant contact with others outside, and to travel as freely as possible. Telephone installation and rental are now too expensive for most pensioners except for a tiny number who qualify for free telephones, and old people are also at the end of the queue when there is a waiting list for new lines. Tens of thousands of people are housebound for simple lack of public transport facilities and the disastrous state of the streets for pedestrians, who can be tripped up by uneven pavements or blocked by a busy road with no safe crossing. Hardly any retired women drive cars. The issue of mobility for old people is a central one for transport policy. It would require pedestrian priority at junctions and across busy roads, safe and reliable public transport, and the maintenance of good pavement surfaces, lighting, and keeping pavements clear of obstacles. This is very much a local authority concern. It has suffered severely from the enormous expenditure by successive governments on cars and lorries at the expense of pedestrians, disregard for road safety measures, and the cuts in Government funding of local and regional authorities for basic maintenance works and public transport. It is very sad that one of the few benefits widely available to pensioners – cheap or free bus passes – has not been funded by central government as an essential service for old people, but taken out of the already dwindling funds available for public transport which is already struggling to maintain basic services. Some Social Service Departments of local Councils offer Dial-A-Ride schemes for disabled people, which are very valuable and should be greatly expanded. But the many people who can

No it's not menopausal depression, it's no pay, no sick leave, no pension, no identity.

walk short distances can be helped simply by improving bus services and pedestrian facilities, which would make all the difference between the misery of being housebound and the independence of being able to get around on your own. Lack of exercise is itself a major contributor to rapid deterioration in physical and mental health.

Activity of all kinds is the key to well-being in old age. It is completely illogical that we should regard planned activities and facilities for children to be an essential use of public funds, while denying the often much cheaper requirements of old people for company and regular activity. Old people's clubs and centres do in fact flourish, up and down the country, but it is a matter of chance whether a particular person who could benefit has one within easy reach, with available space. They do not have to be highly organised from outside, but can in many cases be run by the members with their own resources of time and talents. They can also operate as local centres for services to old people on a practical level, from welfare rights advice to repairs of household goods. They are the obvious place for classes, therapy for depressed or confused people, and voluntary work by the members themselves for the benefit of the whole community. One outstandingly successful experiment, for example, is the 'Foster-grandparenting' scheme throughout the United States, where low-income retired people are given training courses and then placed in homes for disturbed children, on a fixed fee basis, to provide a unique contribution of support and affection for those who have been deprived of both for most of their childhood. The benefit to the volunteers themselves, as well as the children, has been outstanding: both have derived a great boost in their sense of purpose in life and in their own value as individuals. The foster grandparents stay in the job for a remarkably long time; in one survey in Detroit, over half the original trainees were still doing the job ten years later. The women were doing particularly well, using their many years of experience in child-rearing. Similar results have been found with old people who have themselves benefited from group therapy sessions with professionals, developing as counsellors and group leaders in their own right.

A considerable amount of support and help is needed at times of crisis, and too often is unavailable. Practical help may be needed in sorting out the financial affairs of a woman whose husband has just died without involving her in their joint finances. There can be a real crisis over paying for the funeral, with the death grant still at a ludicrously low level. As things now stand, tax and social security systems are loaded against this country's 3 million widows. Many more financial and other practical forms of help need to be made available. At the moment, widows in particular find that the only people likely to show any understanding or sympathy for their problems are other widows, and they have set up self-help and campaigning networks such as Cruse and the National Association of Widows. Even more crucial sometimes is the emotional support and advice which is so important after a bereavement, and this too is often available only on an erratic basis which leaves many of those most in need without any help at all. An emotional crisis over the loss of a husband, relative or friend can easily set off a rapid decline in mental and physical well-being, and the provision of help and support at the right time can prevent or reverse the slide into depression and immobility.

Our widespread belief that decline is inevitable and irreversible, despite the recent research which shows that much can be done to restore people to health, actually forces the people involved into a painful, unproductive and miserable period as a dependent and helpless burden on society which can last for many years. This is what many of us fear when we think of 'growing old'. If there is one thing that can dramatically improve the lives of old people, especially women, it is a much greater awareness of the recent advances of the treatment of aging, and a political commitment to developing these findings in the form of practical programmes of help and self-help for old people. Special exercise programmes can restore muscle tone and strength, relieve incontinence and increase overall fitness. The confusion, lethargy, forgetfulness, irritability and insomnia which so often afflict old people can be reversed in many cases by increasing the intake of protein, vitamins and essential trace elements which have been found to be deficient in the great majority of elderly women. A lot of mental symptoms are the result of the inappropriate use of powerful drugs. A single disability may develop which can be isolated and treated, while the rest of the body remains quite healthy. Each person ages in a different way, with very different rates for the various faculties and parts of the body. A problem with hearing, for example, can too easily be misdiagnosed as 'senility'. Innumerable people have been falsely diagnosed as senile for a variety of misleading symptoms. It has been estimated that less than 1 percent of old people actually develop senile dementia.

Some of the leading researchers into aging consider that it is almost impossible at present to establish what medical changes and impairments are caused by aging itself, because it is so complicated by the patterns of 'misuse, disuse or disease' which are imposed by the way old people live in our society. Women even more than men have such bad eating habits, are so withdrawn from the mainstream of society and lead such abnormally sedentary lives that we do not know the limits of improvement if adequate resources were made available to keep them active and involved, or to treat the symptoms now dismissed as 'normal' in order to restore the sick person to health.

The attitude that pensioners are some kind of burden on society will need to be changed, if their political power is to become strong enough to get control of their fair share of public spending. Increasingly, we shall have to rely on retired people to do much of the unpaid community work which plays a vital part in our overall social services, and is increasingly integrated with professional social service and health work. Retired people, especially women, will have to be seen as important contributors to society, not just dependants on those 'of working age'. It is paradoxical that in order to preserve and strengthen the voluntary sector, it will be necessary for many of those involved – almost all women – to devote at least part of their energies to political campaigning. Their experience in working in the community, and especially among the elderly, makes them uniquely informed about the problems and issues surrounding both the needs of the voluntary sector, and the needs of old people. In this they are far ahead of the men who are now taking almost all the decisions affecting everybody else. They are limited in their understanding by the patterns of life-long employment, cut off from the rest of the community in very specialised jobs, and with far too much emphasis on rather sterile 'management' techniques rather than the human reality they are trying to cope with. The men in power are in great need of a little re-education themselves; what better method than to put them through the women's training course of bringing up children, looking after old people, doing voluntary work in their spare time, knowing how it feels not to have enough money or facilities, and generally becoming involved in the whole community?

While men are on this valuable training course, all the women who have already graduated could take over the management.

Resources

The new interest in how women are affected by aging is becoming accessible in book form. The following provide at least an introduction to the debate:

Prime Time by Helen Franks (Pan, London, 1981), a general survey and morale-booster for women in 'mid-life'.

Change and Choice: Women and middle age, a collection edited by Beatrice Musgrave and Zoe Menell (Peter Owen, London, 1980).

Some of the new research on aging is outlined in contributions to *Looking Ahead: A woman's guide to the problems and joys of growing older*, edited by Lillian Troll, Joan Israel and Kenneth Israel (Prentice-Hall, New Jersey, 1977).

For a description of life as a recipient of society's treatment of illness and disability in old age, see Ellen Newton's *This Bed my Centre* (Virago, London, 1980).

For widows, a wide selection of publications as well as practical help is available from Cruse, National Organisation for the Widowed and their Children, 126 Sheen Road, Richmond, Surrey. There is also a campaigning organisation, the National Association of Widows, Stafford District Voluntary Service Centre, Chell Road, Stafford.

Women looking after elderly relatives are well served by the National Council for Carers and their Elderly Dependants, (address page 105).

There is also of course a vast range of pensioners' organisations and campaigns, on local and national levels: the best contact point is your local library.

12
The Women's Vote

'Women's issues' can no longer be seen as a small number of items confined to home, family and children: everything in the political arena is of interest and concern to women just as much as to men. We certainly have a different perspective, and in many cases we attach different priorities than do men to each of the issues.

The women's vote needs to be considered very carefully by the politicians: it is no longer enough for them to dismiss us as naturally conservative and suspicious of change, which is the current stereotype they impose on us. The Conservative Party tends to take the women's vote for granted, and the Labour Party often seems to have given up on us. Yet while the Conservatives have women much more prominently presented as part of the party, on many issues – equal pay, social security and tax, the NHS and action against discrimination – women's interests have been taken much more seriously by Labour. The Liberals and SDP are erratic, swinging from one extreme – two women on every shortlist – to the other, which is all-male presentations of the party and its media image, reinforced by the double act of David Owen and David Steel.

Yet politicians are apparently aware of the importance of the women's vote: a survey of all MPs just before the 1983 election by *Honey* magazine brought replies from over a third, including the leaders of the Labour and Alliance parties. Wide differences were apparent between MPs of different parties: 83 percent of the Labour MPs who replied wanted free child-care for any parents who wanted it, while 86 percent of the Tories wanted women to be obliged to look after their children on their own. Many of the MPs, while anxious to please, showed a very poor understanding of issues such as rape and domestic violence. There is clearly a big job to be done, in educating our politicians in the facts of a woman's life and relating these to political issues. Only the slowly dawning realisation that women are looking for representatives who will take us seriously, and that some women would be prepared to switch their votes to achieve this, will induce them to make the effort.

Not enough is known about women's voting patterns. Unfortunately the political pollsters have not been very interested in finding out whether we are motivated differently from men when we vote. Few opinion polls are published to show the difference in opinion between women and men, even though it has been recognised that there has always been a 'gender gap' on many issues. A promising exception to this lack of interest was a Marplan poll published in the *Guardian* during February 1983. This showed that the priority attached to different issues varied widely between women and men. Considerably more women thought that the most important issues at the next election would be education, health and social services, and housing – none of these recognised by the main parties as distinctly 'women's issues'. Women were particularly concerned to preserve health, education and welfare programmes from any cuts, even if it meant sacrificing reductions in taxation. Women and men attached the same priority to unemployment and inflation – hitherto seen as men's and women's issues respectively – and to immigration and race relations. More men than women were interested in defence, the EEC, 'law and order' and public ownership, issues which do not have the immediate interest for women that the more urgent issues of social policy have. It is particularly interesting that 'law and order', as presently defined, does not seem to have much appeal to women. Indeed the forms of violence that women face are very inadequately dealt with by the police and courts at the moment, and are not generally included in discussions of law enforcement. The response by women on this issue is completely contrary to the stereotype of women as conservative voters who take a very punitive line on corporal and capital punishment.

It has also been observed in a number of countries that truly right-wing politics – Hitler's Brownshirts, the National Front and other racist or authoritarian movements – are mainly a male phenomenon, with their militaristic style and strong propensity for violence.

It has been claimed many times by political commentators that women are more likely than men to vote for the Conservative Party, and in fact this has become an entrenched idea in political folklore. Yet it may never have been true that an individual woman was more likely to vote Tory than a man of similar background. What may be true is that the preponderance of women among the retired age group, particularly of upper- and middle-class women, means that there are more women not only in the electorate but in the class and age groups most likely to vote Conservative. As early as 1964, the women in the youngest age group were more likely than men to vote Labour. By 1979 there were no more Conservative votes from women than from men – indicating a slight preference among women for the other parties as compared with men, in the younger age-groups. By the 1983 General Election there was a significant trend among all women away from the Tories, compared with men. For the first time ever the Conservative Party drew less support from women than from men – under Britain's first female Prime Minister. The party's campaign, and its record in office, had emphasised increased spending on defence and privatising the social services, while taking a hard line against protecting jobs. The main beneficiaries of women's desertion were the centrist parties, the Liberals and SDP, with women shifting their votes from both Conservative and Labour to a greater extent than the men. Many women seemed to be voting *against* the main parties in a recognisable protest vote, indicating that they saw these parties as having little to offer them which would justify any kind of party loyalty.

The Labour Party, which has a number of policy commitments which could prove very attractive to women, made a serious tactical mistake in its presentation of women's issues in the run-up to the 1983 election campaign. Instead of seeing women as being interested in the entire range of policy, from social services and education to housing and the economy, the party made the classic mistake of supposing that there was a distinct set of 'women's issues' which could be handled by a separate front-bench represen-tative, with the linked proposal to make her Minister of a new Department of Women's Affairs if Labour formed the next government. Joan Lestor was the appointee, and found herself in an impossible position: she was not 'shadowing' any Government department which she could study and criticise in the same way as her other front-bench colleagues; she was also unable to speak on topics she had worked on before, such as education and foreign affairs, since they were not part of her brief. She was reduced to searching out special issues not covered by any of the current political debate: such as whether or not VAT should be charged on sanitary towels – where she met with derision from the largely male

159

House of Commons. It is to be hoped that all the parties, in future, will use their leading women as front-bench representatives for major portfolios – get women's power *into* politics, rather than hive them off into a marginal role in 'women's affairs' as if these were outside the political mainstream.

Political issues are still being defined by the parties almost entirely as men's issues, and women are reduced to choosing among policies that have no direct appeal to our own experience and concerns. Where women's interests *are* taken into account in political debate and action, there can be some profound changes in the way we vote. Already women are voting at the same rate as men, although for many years we participated less in elections than they did. One study of women's voting in the United States, where there is a different set of laws for each State providing a basis for comparison, found that in States with a number of laws already in effect which were favourable to women (on the principle of equal rights, against discrimination in credit, housing and public services, protection in rape cases, and job discrimination) women were more likely to go out and vote. There was no connection at all between these factors and men's interest in voting. This indicates that as political change starts to take account of women's needs there is likely to be a surge of interest among women in the whole question of politics. And obviously, we will be looking for parties and candidates who offer us the best deal, with the greatest credibility.

The women's vote has in fact become suddenly very critical in recent elections, inducing a state of hysteria among some politicians who have never before had to try and deal with it. In the American presidential election of 1980, Ronald Reagan as a candidate of the far right would have lost if only women had been voting: American women were 52 percent against Reagan, while the men voted overwhelmingly for him in a split which was unprecedented in US electoral history – in the previous presidential elections there had been no difference between the voting patterns of women and men. Much of the difference may have been due to the issue of the Equal Rights Amendment to the US Constitution, which Reagan opposed; over 20 percent of women said they would vote according to whether or not the candidate supported the ERA. In the mid-term Congressional elections, women's voting shift towards Democratic candidates was seen as largely responsible for the new composition of a more liberal Congress hostile to Reagan's politics.

160

Recent elections in Britain and Ireland have also produced sudden panics in the political parties as they wake up to the fact that women can be an important political force: this happened in Ireland's 1981 elections, for example, and in the General Election of 1979 in Britain where for the first time there was a woman at the head of a major party. As already mentioned, in the Conservative Party's campaign, enormous stress was placed on Margaret Thatcher doing the shopping, washing up and being with her family: acting just like a 'ordinary' woman, in fact, even though her real life has little in common with most of ours. The Labour Party panicked, not knowing how to counter this powerful image of a woman leader who actually understood ordinary women's lives. Jim Callaghan had to issue grim warnings to men in his party to stop attacking her as 'that woman', 'the bitch' and other reminders of their hostility to women in general, which were handing her a strong sympathy vote. Labour Party leaders had to scurry around to find women for the press conference platforms, for the first time, and the men tried hard to remember what their party was offering to women. Needless to say, Maggie and her advisers won the propaganda battle.

By the 1983 election, however, the emphasis was on her authority as 'the biggest man of them all', and none of the parties made much effort to identify seriously with women. Public debate was almost all between men, with the media making no attempt to balance the discussion with even a few women. Labour's leadership was projected as all-male, as was the Alliance's: possibly a crude reaction to the overwhelming image of the woman Prime Minister treating her male Cabinet colleagues as small boys. Roy Jenkins told one audience that just one woman in politics was 'too much'. There was almost no mention of women's interests in the various issues; instead there was repetition of stale old formulas on both sides. 1983 stands out as the great male 'leadership' election: perhaps the last of its kind?

At the moment women appear in comparison with men, to be voting more on the basis of the personalities than on policies, though the two cannot be easily separated, since particular politicians are seen as standing for particular policies, and voters are interested not just in what the parties promise but in whether the personalities involved can be trusted to deliver the goods. The electorate generally has become very cynical. In the 1983 Marplan poll already mentioned, women were less likely than men to vote mainly on the basis of policies (61 percent compared to 69 percent of men). The factors that influenced women were the personalities of the leaders, the local candidate, and 'traditional loyalty' to a particular party – as distinct from a strong commitment to the party, which was more likely to be found among the men.

Such an approach is necessary for women as long as the parties are not putting over policies relevant to our concerns, or making an effort to convince us that their periodic statements on women are integrated into the top priority programmes that they will carry through, if elected, no matter what. The Labour Party has particular trouble with this, since it produces wonderful statements of policy for women which are forgotten when it comes to the all-important selection of priorities at election time, or to making major policy statements on the key issues. Women make political judgments on the basis of the overall record and philosophy of the parties, not just isolated claims to support women's rights. If there are few women in prominent positions, that obviously has a role in our decision. The well publicised image of a woman as one of the leadership, or as the overall boss, will obviously appeal to women who otherwise feel completely ignored by the politicians and alienated by their policies. We should note that women questioned by Marplan were more likely than the men to describe Margaret Thatcher as 'warm', 'caring' and 'in touch with ordinary people'. A similar phenomenon seems to have operated with Shirley Williams, who in her time has been extremely popular especially among women – because of, not in spite of, her somewhat dishevelled appearance and disorganised air. If the parties are to make any serious impact among women voters they will have to convince us through their presentation of policies, and by allocating responsible public positions to women in the party, that they too could be 'warm', 'caring' and the rest.

Getting organised

Before we consider ways for women to organise politically to get what we want, it is very important for us to recognise the power of the men's organisations. We hardly ever see any mention of these powerful male clubs and networks, both open and semi-secret, which form such important power bases in politics, the trade unions, local government, the civil service and the law as well as in business. They are the real power behind the throne for exclusive groups of men who range from the most privileged – with their clubs in Mayfair and Pall Mall – to those who frequent the

162

Working Men's Clubs which are such important centres in the industrial areas of the North and Midlands.

The men's organisations wield enormous influence over our whole political process by deciding on which candidates and policies to push in the political parties and trade unions. In many cases the influence is anti-democratic and even reactionary, as in the case of the vote-rigging conducted by right-wing groups such as Catholic Action in the trade unions, Labour and Social Democratic Parties.

It is no accident that the Sex Discrimination Act, which was advertised as abolishing discrimination, deliberately allows 'private' clubs and organisations to keep women out, or to discriminate against their women members. The key to such organisations is their all-male club 'atmosphere' in which women's interests can be dismissed and women discussed from a point of view that may be hostile, without any possibility for us to know what is being decided or to participate in the debate. I am reminded of an uncomfortable, very exclusive meeting I attended once about Africa, where not a single African was present although some of the discussions involved a process of policy formation about the continent by some very powerful Europeans and Americans. I was told that Africans would be unwelcome, since they would inhibit the 'club' atmosphere in which their problems were being discussed.

In the United States, where strong action is being taken against a number of companies for discrimination against their women employees, membership of exclusive businessmen's clubs is recognised as essential to gaining key promotions. In the case of the Bank of America, which under pressure from the courts had launched a major programme of positive action to get women into management, it was discovered that the bank was still paying large membership subscriptions, for their male executives only, to exclusive men's clubs. There was great resistance by men in management to halting this practice, and they were finally forced to stop the payments only when the US Treasury threatened to withdraw its contracts.

In Britain the influence of the clubs is even greater than in the United States, particularly for London-based activities and those relating to the Government. Virtually all male civil servants in senior grades of the Foreign Office, the Treasury and other Ministries belong to one or other of these secretive institutions a short walk from Whitehall. Important meetings are held there, often over lunch or drinks, in men-only rooms. Government ministers, if they are men, almost always belong to one or more of the clubs, as do many male Members of Parliament. Judges and top lawyers belong, as do senior police officers. So do senior executives of many big companies and public institutions. Many business deals and offers of top jobs take place in the cosy atmosphere of the all-male clubs. We are dealing here with the 'Establishment', that self-perpetuating group of men, in a variety of senior positions, who meet in secret to determine issues which are rightfully the province of Parliament, the court system, and the open market-place. It is a system which protects unearned and unelected privilege and helps to concentrate wealth and power in a few hands, far from public scrutiny. Few men can join – they would have to have the right 'connections' to start with. No woman can ever join. The excuse is that it would spoil 'the atmosphere'.

An even more secretive system of men's clubs is the network of Freemasons, that apparently anachronistic mumbo-jumbo organisation which in fact wields quite excessive influence over public and business life. In some industries, including nationalised bodies like the Post Office as well as certain hospitals, trade unions and other public institutions, promotion to the senior ranks may depend on membership of the appropriate Freemasons' lodge, open of course to men only. Some areas of small business, such as jewellers and the liquor trade, are closely controlled by branches of the Masons who make sure that big contracts are channelled to their members – all of them men. With members of the Royal Family among its patrons, the Freemasons' network is dealing in some very valuable public business as well as practising systematic discrimination between members and non-members, in defiance of basic principles of fairness and openness in financial dealings which we like to think characterise our society. Membership is very broad and influence is wielded most particularly in the business world, in local government and in the Conservative Party. There have been a number of cases coming to light of corrupt deals being worked out between local Council officials, key Councillors and local businessmen who make a handsome living from local authority contracts – all those involved meeting through the local Freemasons' lodge.

Would it solve women's problems to get access to these men's clubs and networks? It is completely wrong in principle to perpetuate such elitism and secrecy; women's concerns, in fact everybody's, should be the subject of open debate and public accountability for important decisions. The ease with which powerful male institutions can intimidate the 'token' women they allow in is now all too obvious from our experience of this phenomenon in politics and employment.

Simply being a member of an organisation is no guarantee of fair treatment within it. Women can belong to the Conservative Party, but are kept out of many local Conservative clubs. Discrimination against women members is a basic principle of the Working Men's Clubs, which comprise over 4,000 separate institutions all over the country with a total membership of 4 million. In many places the club is the social centre for the whole community, and whole families are often members or associates. It is often the place where the latest information and gossip circulates and local politics and trade business is discussed, and strategies worked out. As with practically all voluntary associations, the clubs depend on women's unpaid work in organising activities and raising funds. Yet the Club and Institute Union, to which all these clubs belong, makes women second-class members. We are not allowed to be on a management committee, to hold any office or to represent the club as delegates to the annual policy conference. Clubs often have rooms where we are not allowed, special events for men only, and even white lines painted on the floor which women are not supposed to cross – especially where there are snooker tables or other club facilities. We are not allowed to introduce new members, and most important of all we do not get the CIU card which entitles the men to go into any other club. A strong campaign against this discrimination, the Equal Rights in Clubs Campaign for Action (ERICCA), has faced some violent abuse from some of the men involved in the club movement, who have been especially aggressive about women's attempt to speak as elected club delegates at the annual CIU conference.

The men's organisations generally represent a powerful force for discrimination which is so far untouched by the Sex Discrimination Act. The EOC has in fact proposed an amendment to the Act to make it illegal for clubs to discriminate against their own members who are women – although there is no attempt in this to outlaw all-male clubs as such. Much more attention needs to be paid now to the London clubs, the Freemasons and also the men-only business groups like the Rotary Clubs. Ostensibly for 'social' or charitable purposes, they are widely recognised, and attract members, as the place to make all the right contacts and get ahead of everybody else as a result.

As long as men get together in an exclusive club which depends on keeping women out, we shall need to organise against them in our own search for equality of opportunity. In organisations which depend on our support but give special privileges to their male members, there will be a hard struggle to eliminate this discrimination which may be part of the custom and practice of the whole thing since its beginning. And of course, we need to get organised as women in order to make this challenge.

Organising for what?

Obviously women have political differences, and we have different interests and aspirations depending on our circumstances – just as men do. But what is immediately evident when you look at women's political attitudes is the number of issues on which most of us can agree. The programmes of women's organisations all across the country, local and national, traditional and feminist, all tend to converge on certain key issues, even where they disagree on many others. In November 1980 almost 100 of these organisations representing more than 2 million members, came together under the title 'Women's Action' to agree on eight points of direct concern to the majority of women which need parliamentary action during the 1980s. They decided to back candidates who promised to vote for or actively support measures that would contribute to the following aims:

Higher, index-linked child benefits.

Flexible working hours for both sexes, with adequate leave for child sickness or family emergencies; the right for parents of either sex to take time off to raise a family without losing their jobs, seniority or pension rights.

Creche and nursery facilities for all who wish to use them; after-school and holiday care where needed.

Equal pay for work of equal value. Individual taxation for everyone.

The same retirement age for men and women, flexible for both.

An education policy that provides equal opportunity for girls and boys alike and encourages girls to achieve their full potential.

The inclusion of representative groups of women on all housing, town planning and environmental committees.

Maternity, gynaecological and family planning services that meet women's real needs.

There is an immense programme of social and financial reform which could keep legislators busy for a considerable time, if enough pressure was brought to bear by women getting politically organised to push for it.

It is important also for us to know that these proposals are not seriously opposed by the men. In 1977 the *Observer* conducted an interesting survey among its readers. It showed very strong support by men, almost as many as women, for a fairer deal on equal pay, income tax and social security issues, including the invalid care allowance and the notorious 'cohabitation rule'. There was strong support for women's right to control pregnancy and childbirth, the right to anonymity in rape trials and to protection from domestic violence; there was also general agreement that women staying at home with children were doing a job as important as men in paid employment. The sample was obviously biased towards more liberal and middle-class people, and it may be that some opposition on these issues might be found in other sections of the population – but all the indications are that many of the men would be happy to see women getting a fair deal. It is largely a matter of getting the same degree of political priority attached to the changes we want to see as are now given to the men's main concerns (on which they are probably far more divided). Only women can provide the necessary impetus.

How should women organise politically?

There have for many decades now been separate women's organisations within political parties to recruit women into the work and to push for women's interests to be recognised by the party as a whole. This was particularly true of the Labour Party and the allied Co-op Party, an offshoot of the co-operative movement which has always been very much identified with the concerns of women, and relied almost totally on women's support in their commitment to co-op shops and services. In both cases, it was militant women who set up the women's sections of the Labour Party and the Co-operative Women's Guild; they later fell into an auxiliary role to the rest of the party activities, becoming identified with the tea-making and the jumble sales, but providing a ready-made network of influence for the recent wave of feminists entering the parties. It is a great pity that the network of co-op shops and services has been virtually taken over by young men highly educated in the ethos of managerial power and of 'rationalisation'; they have slashed the network of smaller co-op stores, cut the links between members and their shops, and left many of the traditional working-class areas without any contact with the co-operative movement at all. They have destroyed in a few years an enormously strong women's movement that parallelled the largely male-dominated trade union movement within the overall labour tradition. The future of the co-operative movement looks bleak at the moment, and women are politically much poorer as a result.

Other organisations set up by leading feminists after winning the vote have survived much better, although they too now need to reassess their political position in the face of a large but declining membership, and the need for a higher profile to attract younger women. The large women's organisations such as the Women's Institutes, Townswomen's Guilds, and the women's church organisations have for a long time campaigned on a wide range of issues, under the pretence that they are 'non-political' organisations. What they in fact mean is simply that they are not involved in party politics. However, like many other campaigning organisations they feel under constant threat from the erratic rulings of the Charity Commissioners on what is or is not political, and the strange distinctions made between education about issues, which is a charitable activity, and doing something about them, which is not. The sooner our charity laws are brought up to date, the better it will be for the big women's organisations.

Many of these bodies are the direct descendants of the women's suffrage movement of the late nineteenth and early twentieth centuries. Since the 1920s many of the activists from that movement have worked hard through these organisations at political and general education among women, with their network of active groups throughout the country in rural as much as in urban areas. They now represent millions of women; work hard on policy formulation within the organisations themselves; are regularly consulted by government departments on a wide range of legislative issues; and are respected as extremely well informed on everything they get involved in, as well as a source of nominations for women to serve on official bodies of all kinds. Their political interests range from transport to health and safety,

168

to housing, to crime, to education, to almost anything. They take a strikingly liberal view of these issues, in contrast to their popular press image as conservative organisations, resisting change. Their problems, apart from the need to keep up a 'non-political' style for the Charity Commissioners, lie in the derision accorded them by much of the national press, which regularly scoffs at their annual conferences, and the difficulty of recruiting the increasing numbers of women with two jobs – one paid and the other not – which leaves no time for regular meetings.

The women's organisations are in fact at a crossroads: their membership is falling because of the dwindling numbers of women with free time and energy. Although the organisations are greatly respected by Ministers and civil servants who work with them on issues, they receive very little public recognition. They are attempting to compensate for the low priority given to women's views in the major political parties by putting forward their views in a non-party context; yet the most active younger women are unlikely to be getting involved to provide a continuing input of new energies for this work. It seems vital that the work the women's organisations are doing should be given more recognition and support, and that their expertise in presenting the women's point of view should be recognised by the major parties and used as a resource in their own policy-making process, both in and out of government. The WI has indeed in 1983 launched a major effort to recapture its campaigning tradition.

The parties' women's sections do in fact participate directly in the National Council of Women (NCW) which is unusual in its overtly campaigning stance: the suffragist founders decided at the beginning not to accept the constraints of charitable status. It has its own national network of groups working on both local and national issues, and also has affiliated women's organisations ranging from the political parties to the completely non-political church women's groups. The NCW in fact offers a way in to the political debate for women which is very flexible: anyone can form a local branch, and it can immediately send representatives to the special policy committees at regional or national level. As a way of learning formal meetings procedure and public speaking, this and other women's organisations are a very useful training ground. For anyone wanting to have an effective input into conventional politics, procedure is in fact vitally important. Operating according to standard rules saves a vast amount of time, energy and aggravation.

Growing up alongside the traditional women's organisations in recent years have been a new generation of single-issue women's networks which serve a practical function, a training role and a national policy-making role at the same time. One very successful example is the Pre-School Playgroups Association, with over 100,000 groups involving almost half a million women with small children in a mixture of self-help and campaigning work which includes dealings with local and national government. It started with the overwhelming response of women to a letter in the Women's Page of the *Guardian* in 1961. Another organisation produced by a kind of spontaneous combustion in the 1960s is the National Housewives' Register – also started by a letter to the same Women's Page. It particularly attracted women who were not members of anything else, but were feeling isolated and depressed and needed a group to get involved in. It is impossible to estimate the range of other organisations, campaigns and pressure groups run wholly or mainly by women, and which sprang up in the sixties and seventies to campaign on particular issues at local as well as national level, some very stable and some existing for a particular purpose such as campaigning to keep a nursery school open or fight the menace of heavy lorries or a new road scheme. The involvement of women in community politics and local issues generally, on a very wide range of issues, has to be recognised as an indication of the energy and motivation which is available for politics generally.

It should be a short step, then, for women to become involved in more than one issue at a time, and through the organisations which – whether we like it or not – are central to the resolution of local as well as national issues: the political parties. It is important for women to understand how the parties work, especially at the local level which is where we have to begin. The parties do not just select candidates and organise for them in local and national elections, important though that is. They are also deeply involved in the life of the community by nominating their members to the Boards of Governors of schools, local charities and other organisations. They also nominate many of the magistrates and, where appropriate, prison visitors. From a purely opportunist point of view, any woman who is already active in local issues should consider joining a party for the access it provides to some of the apparently non-political institutions in the community. There may well be pressure to stick to making tea and running the jumble sales – but nobody can force us into that job if we prefer the avenues into real politics which are open to party members. In fact many women are very good at organising things that a local party needs done, and we might in some circumstances use that as a bargaining counter to get access to the more influential positions within the party. There are women now coming into the major parties, particularly the Labour and Alliance parties, who have a deliberate strategy of voting for other women in contested positions as well as making sure that women's issues are included in the internal debates and the public presentation of policies. Efforts to arrange babysitting rotas have been started, to cut through the pattern of men coming to meetings and women staying at home. It is, if you like, a form of entryism.

One of the difficult problems for women in the parties is that of getting women to be candidates for election, for local and national government. Many men would like us to think that they are uniquely qualified to represent our interests. They would have us believe that putting women forward for winnable seats means a one-issue candidate, a loser, and something that is not a high priority compared with the bread-and-butter issues which concern everybody, not just women. It is well worth remembering, though, that factions within political parties have always manoeuvred to get their candidate accepted by the party as a whole, as the best way of advancing their cause. Selecting women as candidates is important – not as an end in itself, but as a vital means to the end of getting reasonable priority for our interests.

One obvious question is whether *any* woman would be better than a man, or whether a 'token woman' would be worse. Many would point to our first woman Prime Minister as an object lesson in what to avoid if women's issues are to be helped rather than hindered. Margaret Thatcher has certainly, in many respects, been more 'masculine' in her politics than most men, and scornful of other women's problems. She has said quite openly that women should be persuaded to give up their jobs when they have children (although she made no attempt to do this herself) and has shown very little sympathy for the problems of child care, low income and the care of dependent relatives which her Government's policies have made worse. Margaret Thatcher is an extreme case, however, and even she showed a sudden understanding of a women's issue when, after some very questionable court judgments on convicted rapists, she ordered that the number of judges allowed to take rape cases should be strictly limited to those with the necessary experience and sound judgment. Most women in political life, however hostile towards women less fortunate than themselves, have sooner or later shown an understanding of women's issues which marks them out from the men. In the United States Congress, it has been observed that the women of all backgrounds and political parties are distinctly different from men, more liberal and more prepared to take strong positions on issues of principle which might jeopardise their careers. For example, most of them have favoured registration of firearms in the teeth of the powerful gun lobby, something that most of the men do not dare to tackle. They have generally supported social services and have been unimpressed with prestige projects favoured by the men, such as motorway building and huge new military programmes. A study of women in the British House of Lords shows them to work harder than men, and to concern themselves with social issues such as health and education rather than defence.

In Britain the small group of women in the House of Commons, where they have never constituted as many as 5 percent of the MPs, has been immensely important in pushing for new social programmes and legislation that particularly benefit women, even though several of them had very little interest in women when they were elected. The best known of these is perhaps Barbara Castle, who always insisted on keeping away from 'women's issues' but campaigned tirelessly for equal pay between women and men.

In the battle against the Corrie Bill which aimed to restrict women's access to abortion, it was the small group of Labour women in the House – with very little backing from the men in their party despite the fact that this is official party policy – who organised its defeat. On the other hand, some of the Conservative women were supporting Corrie. It would seem that virtually any woman is likely to support some of the issues of particular concern to women, some of the time, but if you want a candidate you can rely on, the selection has to be done carefully to find a candidate with a proven record of working for women on all issues. Overall this is getting easier, and women standing as potential candidates are more likely now than they used to be to give priority to women's interests. Since the mid-1970s it has been noticeable that women MPs have become increasingly assertive about women's demands, the most important so far being abortion.

In local government, too, women have played an important role despite their small numbers, which are better than at national level but still inadequate: around 15 percent to 20 percent, and in some places falling. In spite of this, there has been a new spirit of cohesion among women on local Councils, where they have formed an effective group within their parties and won a number of concessions for women. Several Labour Councils now have special Women's Committees which have taken up a range of issues including housing, social services, education and youth work. The Women's Committee of the Greater London Council has obtained a budget of several million pounds, much of which is being spent on additional nursery facilities and the rest on direct support for women's organisations and activities of practically every kind. It has bought a building for the specific use of A Woman's Place and the Women's Research and Resources Centre, and provided a meeting-place at County Hall for many women's conferences and meetings. Women's Committees in some of the Labour boroughs have worked on a smaller but very useful scale: Camden, for example, has worked hard on the prostitution laws as they affect the borough, and Southwark has held a series of meetings with women on Council estates. The work is often very controversial, with the press making constant attacks particularly on the grants to women's groups, but for once women are working out some of the newest and most exciting possibilities in local government. Even where there is no strong women's group on a local Council, women working as individual Councillors can have considerable scope for helping women and women's groups in the community; many of the issues discussed in this book are within the scope of local authority action. Case work, too, offers an opportunity for helping individuals with a wide range of their problems, personal as well as strictly political.

The selection of candidates, which is one of the crucial issues in party politics, can sometimes be bitterly contested. Some of the men like to suggest that having a woman stand is risking votes for the party, although detailed studies of voting patterns for female and male candidates for the same party show no overall difference, and no parliamentary seat has been won or lost by a party because the candidate was a woman or man. There are some minimal shifts in certain circumstances, but they are as likely to give women the advantage as men. If some of the electorate were to start voting systematically for women wherever possible, it would become a positive advantage to start putting up substantial numbers of women as candidates. The idea current among some of the old guard that there are no women available to stand is belied by the very large numbers of women standing in seats where their party has no realistic chance of winning – Labour women in seats with huge Tory majorities, and vice versa. Many of them make great efforts to get out all possible votes, efforts which might have little effect in the seats where they are standing and should be put to use in the marginal or – even better – the safe seats. Where women have stood and won, it is almost entirely in marginal seats where they are then vulnerable to swings away from their party. In the 1979 General Election, which brought in our much-publicised woman Prime Minister, the number of women in Parliament fell substantially because Labour women, the great majority of women in the House, were concentrated in the highly marginal seats that were lost in the national swing to the Tories. More Labour women were lost in 1983, with Tory women outnumbering them for the first time since Nancy Astor's solitary reign; the total number of women was just one more than before the election. The Liberal group of MPs, and the smaller SDP, were strictly Men Only.

Constituency parties which operate in safe seats have a special responsibility to replace some of their excessive numbers of men with women, if the many women standing as candidates are not to waste all their efforts but form a reasonable-sized group in Parliament. The party overall would need to have a good number of women in its parliamentary group from which to draw women into the leadership: this is essential if the party overall is to project a balanced image that will not repel women. The Labour Party suffers more than the others from its image of massed ranks of male delegates, at trade union as well as party conferences and public events; this blunts its ability to persuade women that, in policy terms, Labour has more to offer than the others.

Perhaps the big question for women, if we are prepared to get our hands dirty by getting involved in a political party, is – which one? It is really not possible to remain uncommitted. The 300 Group, which aims to get many more women into Parliament, is trying to do this by recruiting women prepared to stand and *then* getting them into a party. This is completely the wrong way around, and shows a lack of understanding about the way politics works, at least in this country. Nobody, woman or man, will have any impact in a party – with the possible exception of the SDP – unless they are committed to the party and its policies, and actively engaged in the debates going on inside it. The best way for women to start is to become active in the nitty-gritty workings of the party as quickly as possible, preferably by taking some responsibility for its organisation, and wherever possible to participate in a women's section as a focus for getting our issues high up the list of party priorities.

When women begin to make a significant impact, the battle can become very heated if there are men who are unwilling to share power and position with us. This happens particularly on the right and left wings of all the parties. The right-wingers are prone to organising in their male clubs and private meetings which we are not supposed to know about. They are quite prepared to defy the party rules, including refusing to admit members who disagree with their 'line', bussing in people from outside, and other dirty tricks. The efforts to eliminate this kind of manipulation in the Labour Party, making representatives much more accountable for their actions to the party members, have led to enormous upheavals particularly as the old guard has allies in the press who will denounce their critics as 'Militants' or 'Trotskyists' when in many cases they are neither.

Left-wing men, too, can be decidedly unfriendly towards the idea of involving women. The influx of women into the Labour Party, with strong demands for a more feminist approach, has been countered by some of the more sectarian men who have great difficulty with this on a personal level. At the 1982 Women's Conference of the Labour Party, for example, militant delegates combined with right-wing trade unionists in attacking the proposals for women to have direct representation on the National Executive Committee and the right to put their resolutions directly to the annual Party Conference. In response to the women's demands for priority to be given to women as candidates in order to correct the imbalance in Parliament, Chris Mullin of *Tribune* fame wrote primly: 'Personally I would favour positive discrimination in favour of socialists.' The clear implication is that women are less likely to be proper socialists than men.

Women are often less pretentious in our claims to ideological purity of whatever variety than many of the self-styled leaders, the men. We have a practical programme of action to carry out, and the finer details of theoretical politics are of much less interest to us than to the men whose leadership is now in question. Upheaval within political parties, especially the Labour Party at the moment, can be a symptom of major changes being demanded from within which upset the old, male bastions of power, and could mean the eventual emergence of a more balanced, more democratic party. Only time will tell whether the old guard or the new will win.

The other parties conduct less public battles. In the SDP the strong demand for women's issues and candidates to be given an equal place with the men's suffered a series of heavy defeats as the men who defected from other parties seized the key positions for themselves. Women seem to be making little headway in the Conservative Party, where the leading men continue to pontificate about their idealised 'family' as the basis for our future. The Liberals have to a large extent been taken over by the SDP. You pays your money, and you takes your choice. The most important thing to remember is that politics is about power, not ideals. All the parties are dominated by internal debates about policies, and in this forum it is the best-organised who win. For women to be too meek and unwilling to organise within the parties means that we will be left campaigning for policies and candidates with little relevance to us. We should be getting involved as policy-makers in our own right, not *just* as loyal supporters of the men.

There have been many mistakes by women in the political arena, and many defeats for our interests which our possession of the vote has not been adequately protecting. Having a vote is not enough without a clear sense of what it should be used *for*, together with an effective organisation or network to start pushing for what we want through the existing policy-making machinery. We should learn from the experience of the women's suffrage movement, which virtually collapsed as a militant force after winning their big demand of votes for women. Those over 30 got the vote in 1918, and on the same basis as men – over 21 – in 1927. Immediately after the First World War there was an attempt to set up a Women's Party, with many of the leaders of the movement standing unsuccessfully as independent candidates in the 'coupon election', the only one to receive Lloyd George's coalition coupon being Christabel Pankhurst, who lost by a narrow margin. The Women's Party faded away, and attempts to resurrect the idea of a separate party for women, which would somehow be above 'ordinary' politics, have got nowhere. Independent candidates have less and less chance of election, even in the smallest local contests. Those women who have achieved real legislative gains for women have almost all reached Parliament and sometimes Cabinet positions through their parties (the obvious exception was the Independent MP Eleanor Rathbone, but she had no chance of a well deserved Cabinet position because she was not a member of party).

Women have always been political beings, disagreeing violently about many issues as well as having common ground on others.

Our interests cannot be separated from those involving the whole population. In the women's suffrage movement there were arguments over strategy and tactics: the importance of the vote compared with organising in the trade unions and elsewhere, the importance of working-class issues and the battle for votes for working-class men, and the big issue of the First World War – whether to support the war effort or not. There were disputes too about what the vote was intended to achieve. These sorts of political arguments are just as important today, and they are an essential part of women's political participation, to be worked out through politics in its widest sense, whether through political parties or any other kind of political organisation or campaign.

One of the issues which women have in a special sense made our own, is peace and disarmament, particularly in relation to nuclear weapons. This too is a party-political issue: the Conservatives are pushing Cruise missiles and Trident, an 'independent' British nuclear capacity closely related to American use of nuclear missile bases in this country. The Alliance is deeply split, with Liberal policy being against nuclear weapons in Britain but the SDP being in favour provided there is some form of dual control. The Labour Party is now against Cruise missiles and Trident and officially in favour of unilateral nuclear disarmament, although it is well known that Labour Governments in office have taken a line closer to that of the Conservatives. Within each party, except perhaps the Tories, a fierce debate is going on, not only about formal party policy but also about prospects of implementing it if the party wins power. Women are deeply involved, both inside and outside the parties themselves.

The issue has been highlighted as one in which women are particularly interested because of the Women's Peace Camp outside the American nuclear base at Greenham Common, the intended site for Cruise missiles. The women involved have aroused enormous popular support for their stand. A 73-year-old woman sent to prison for demonstrating on missile silos and then refusing to be bound over to 'keep the peace' spoke for many when she accused the Government of planning a third and final World War:

I am protesting at the insanity of the world in letting this happen. I felt compelled to take this action for the sake of future generations.

Opinion polls have consistently shown fewer women than men to be committed to high levels of defence spending, especially on nuclear weapons. We have had minimal knowledge or contact with military affairs generally and feel personally threatened by weapons which are aimed at civilians on both sides: they promise a scale of casualties and destruction that would effectively destroy our whole world even if the politicians and generals survive in their bunkers. Women's issues are by no means confined to the small-scale or the domestic, as has so often been supposed by the policy-makers. Organising for nuclear disarmament through CND and other peace groups has become a major focus for many women who have never before belonged to a political organisation or campaign. The energy and commitment now going into disarmament is providing a crash course in politics and political organising for many of the women involved. Other issues of principle in which many women are active – human rights, relations with Third World countries, and the issues of race relations and citizenship in this country – also involve inevitable encounters with the broader political system.

Women at the crossroads

Women are in a much stronger position now than after the First World War, when we first got the vote: we have more education, better jobs, less overt discrimination and smaller families. For this we owe a huge debt to the women who continued the fight between the two world wars – as individuals, as members of political parties and organisations, and through the big women's organisations. On top of this there has been an enormous shift in public attitudes about women's rights, especially among women, which is largely due to the militant feminist movement of the 1970s. Some feminists are anxious, however, about the possibility of another collapse of militancy for this 'second wave', which could parallel that of the first wave of the women's suffrage movement. Many of those involved have seen the feminist movement become too introverted, too exclusive, riven by disputes, and the surge of energy created by consciousness-raising apparently being dissipated. The women's movement has not given any importance to formal political organisation, which distinguishes it from many of the early militants who saw the vote as the key to political achievement. The difference has been explained in terms of the libertarian or even anarchist philosophy of the feminist movement, arising as it did in the late sixties out of the rejection of established organisations and values which characterised many movements of that time. A great deal of the energy has been devoted to working out alternative life-styles.

It is impossible to separate out the personal from the political, and many radical feminists would see the creation of alternative women's networks, distinct from the old male parties and campaigns, as the best form of political action. It avoids the endless compromises and battles with men that are typical in mainstream politics, and in many of the single-issue groups as well. And we know that alternative forms of organisation, with less emphasis on leadership and on hierarchy, can not only be very rewarding but also have an enormous impact on public opinion – as the women-only peace camp at Greenham Common has shown us. Maybe there will always be a place for women to organise separately, inside and outside conventional party politics and campaigns.

At the same time, though, many of the women who have been involved in the feminist movement and gained enormous impetus and experience from it are now joining the political parties, as a way forward and as a means of re-establishing contact with all women rather than a self-selected feminist vanguard. Politics is not the whole answer to women's aspirations, obviously, and much remains to be worked out between women and men on a personal and family basis. But as long as there are such strong legal and financial pressures on all of us to conform to a male politician's view of society and the family, there will be no real possibility of working out our personal problems in isolation from political activity.

Perhaps the most crucial of all feminist ideas is contained in the slogans: THE PERSONAL IS POLITICAL and THE POLITICAL IS PERSONAL. We cannot retreat into purely personal activities in work, education, child care, health, personal relationships, retirement or any other facet of our lives as long as we are at the sharp end of policies which cut child care, women's pension rights, social security payments, job opportunities and wages, and as long as we are paying out more than our fair share of taxes, doing more 'community care' and missing out on programmes of public investment or public services geared to the interests of men, their needs, their career patterns, their daily lives, their attitudes towards us and their blinkered view of the world as a whole.

The first great wave of the women's movement saw large

numbers of women devoting their lives to seizing the right to participate in politics, through the symbol of the vote. The mass imprisonment, hunger strikes, brutal force-feeding and constant confrontations with authorities, which were not accountable to women in any way, finally won us this basic political right. We must now learn to use political involvement to its full effect, if our interests are ever to be given equal weight with the men's. The militants of the early women's movement were not afraid to fight for what they wanted. We owe it to them, and even more to ourselves, to do the same.

Resources

To join a local branch of one of the political parties, if you do not know anybody who belongs, write to the head office and they will put you in touch with the local Secretary. Be warned: it can take a long time but usually works in the end. Some addresses are:

Conservative and Unionist Party, 32 Smith Square, London SW1;
Labour Party, 150 Walworth Road, London SE17 (they will ask which trade union you are in: some local branches are very keen on you being a member 'if appropriate');
Liberal Party, 1 Whitehall Place, London SW1;
Social Democratic Party, 4 Cowley Street, London SW1;
Communist Party, 16 St. John Street, London EC1.

An important issue is the appointment of women to public bodies and committees of all kinds. This is discussed fully in *Simple Steps to Public Life* by Pamela Anderson, Mary Stott and Fay Weldon (Virago, London, 1980), price £1.50. It includes a very useful list of addresses of women's campaigning organisations. The Equal Opportunities Commission for Northern Ireland is keeping a 'Talent Bank' for public appointments. Its address is Lindsay House, Callender Street, Belfast.

The National Council of Women is at 34 Lower Sloane Street, London SW1; the National Federation of Women's Institutes at 39 Eccleston Street, London SW1; and the National Union of Townswomen's Guilds at 2 Cromwell Place, London SW7.

The Equal Rights in Clubs Campaign for Action (ERRICA) can be contacted c/o 13 Potter Avenue, Lupset, Wakefield, Yorkshire.

There is a detailed review of women's voting patterns, as well as other questions about our political involvement in general, in

Vicky Randall's *Women and Politics* (Macmillan paperback, London, 1982). Voting in the 1983 election was examined by Ivor Crewe in the *Guardian* of 13 June 1983, based on a BBC Gallup survey. *Honey* magazine survey of MPs was published in its July 1983 edition.

The House of Lords survey is by Gavin Drewry and Jenny Brock: *The Impact of Women on the House of Lords*, 1983. Available from the Centre for the Study of Public Policy, University of Strathclyde, Glasgow 1, price £2.

A history of women's record in politics, from the suffrage movement onwards, is provided in Margaret Stacey and Marion Price's *Women, Power, and Politics* (Tavistock Publications, London, 1981).

Casey Miller and Kate Swift
The Handbook of Non-sexist Writing
Revised British edition

A practical book, using hundreds of examples to show
how certain words have come to acquire particular
'gender' meanings; how we can recognise them; and how,
with very little effort, we can use English without
obscuring 'the actions, the contributions and sometimes
the very presence of women'.

Language/Women's Studies   198 × 126   128pp   bibliography
index   3878 5   £3.25

Dale Spender & Elizabeth Sarah, editors
Learning to Lose
Sexism and Education

An anthology of recent feminist research showing how
our education system stacks the cards against girls from
the beginning.

Education/Women's Studies   198 x 126   216pp   3863 7   £3.25

Angela Davis
Women, Race and Class

One of the most brilliant and courageous women of our
generation confronts issues that have haunted feminist
history for over 100 years. Deals with the history of black
women under slavery, working women in industrial
societies, and shows how deeply both racism and sexism
are rooted in class oppression.

Women's Studies   198 × 126   276pp   3892 0   £4.95

Elizabeth Robins
The Convert
Introduced by Jane Marcus

This readable and satisfying Edwardian novel brings to life
the exciting moment in British history when women were
struggling for the right to vote. It is a story told from the
inside, from the author's own life. 'It is also a funny, moving
and beautifully structured novel' Jane Marcus

Fiction/Women's Studies   197 × 130   320pp   3856 4   £2.95